COPING WITH FAILURE

STUDIES IN RHETORIC/COMMUNICATION
Carroll C. Arnold, *Series Editor*

Richard B. Gregg
Symbolic Inducement and Knowing:
A Study in the Foundations of Rhetoric

Richard A. Cherwitz and James W. Hikins
Communication and Knowledge:
An Investigation in Rhetorical Epistemology

Herbert W. Simons and Aram A. Aghazarian, Editors
Form, Genre, and the Study of Political Discourse

Walter R. Fisher
Human Communication as Narration:
Toward a Philosophy of Reason, Value, and Action

David Bartine
Early English Reading Theory:
Origins of Current Debates

Coping with Failure:
THE THERAPEUTIC USES OF RHETORIC

by David Payne

University of South Carolina Press

Published in Columbia, South Carolina, by the
University of South Carolina Press

First Edition

Manufactured in the United States of America

Library of Congress Cataloging-in-Publication Data

Payne, David, 1952–
  Coping with failure.

  (Studies in rhetoric/communication)
  Bibliography: p.
  Includes index.
  1. Rhetoric—Psychological aspects. 2. Failure
(Psychology) 3. Identity (Psychological)
4. Communication—Psychological aspects. I. Title.
II. Series.
P301.5.P75P39 1989   809   88–26145
ISBN 0-87249-593-0

The problem of evil, that is to say the reconciling of our failures, even the purely physical ones, with creative goodness and power, will always remain one of the most disturbing mysteries of the universe for both our hearts and minds.

—Teilhard de Chardin

The greatest mystery is not that we should have been flung at random amid the profusion of life and the stars, but that in what Pascal calls our prison, we can draw from ourselves images powerful enough to deny our nothingness.

—André Malraux

CONTENTS

Contents

EDITOR'S FOREWORD

Almost two decades ago a degree candidate presented her doctoral committee with a rhetorical analysis of several psychotherapists' verbal exchanges with patients. One of the psychotherapists she studied was a member of the committee. The psychological school of thought to which he was most closely allied was the behavior modification school. At the end of the committee's examination and approval of the dissertation, the psychotherapist said to the candidate, "I have learned something here. You tell me I am an effective 'debater' with my clients. That's something I never before thought about my work. I hope for my clients' sakes that you are right, and I shall hereafter watch that dimension of my work. I thank you for your insights." The candidate continues in her explorations of rhetorical dimensions of therapeutic discourse. She would agree, however, that had she two decades ago had the benefit of Professor David Payne's inquiry, she could have been even more incisive in showing the psychotherapist the rhetorical nature of his professional communication.

Until late in this century rhetoric has been treated as the theory and practice of persuasive, public, verbal expression. In the latter half of the century this conception has been considerably broadened under the influence of writings by such theorist-critics as Kenneth Burke, Richard M. Weaver, and Ch. Perelman. Nonetheless, a vision of rhetoric as *publicly* addressed still dominates the majority of today's writings about rhetorical theory and practice. That we do address ourselves and persuade ourselves is granted, but the forms and qualities of that address have been minimally explored.

In *Coping with Failure: The Therapeutic Uses of Rhetoric,* David Payne treats the role of rhetoric uniquely. He is concerned with rhetoric motivated by senses of inadequacy, whether addressed to the self *or* to the public. He argues that such discourse is psychologically and logically prior to motivating people toward "success." Payne is a pioneer in seeking to discover the thematic content, the structural form, and the rhetorical objectives of effective responses to senses of inadequacy. From studying general literature and "self-help" therapies and from exploring the psychological, logical, and social characteristics of "helping" schemes,

Payne believes he has discerned fundamental characteristics of private or public discourse aimed at ameliorating human shortcomings. In this he moves beyond but remains consistent with major insights offered by Aristotle, Cicero, Kenneth Burke, Richard Weaver, Ch. Perelman, Henry W. Johnstone, Jr., and other leading commentators on the philosophical nature of rhetoric.

Psychological treatments of senses of failure have sometimes been referred to as "talking cures." By focusing on the qualities of such talk, Payne identifies the fundamental themes and ends that such discourse does and must treat rhetorically if the "cure" is to soften disappointments. He shows us the basic substance, structure, and purposes of discourse that "heals." By doing so, he equips inquirers into the nature of "helping discourse" with more systematic methods of inquiry and clearer evaluative standards than have been available prior to his book's appearance.

Carroll C. Arnold
Editor, *Rhetoric/Communication*
University of South Carolina Press

PREFACE

This book examines failure as a life situation in which the viability of one's identity comes into question or is destroyed. In this situation communication is addressed to the contingent status of one's identity; communication functions to defend, repair, or change that identity. In address to failure we can observe how the rhetoric of self operates.

Viewing symbolic acts in the ways they address the human situation of failure generates a particular rhetorical perspective on social communication and individual identity. In this book I examine a broad variety of examples to demonstrate that various speeches, dramas, literatures, philosophical treatises, and scientific pleadings of public discourse function by addressing the sense of failure that individuals commonly experience, and that this fact elucidates the motivational logic of those discourses. Through the critical examination of these various documents and media, I seek to present the central tenets of a therapeutic theory of rhetoric. This theory is founded upon traditional rhetorical-poetic ideas of the functions of discourse, and in many ways builds upon the communication theories of Kenneth Burke. I have sought to make relevant extensions and applications of these perspectives to what I believe to be pressing issues of communication study today.

Individual success and failure appear to be the most shared, if not the most important, contemporary standards for evaluating the worth and relevance of virtually any issue. Further, we evaluate worth and relevance with reference to our individual "identities" and the potential impact that events will have upon their success and failure. "Identity" is a rhetorical project in which most persons are actively engaged. We demand that our enterprises and institutions offer the possibility of individual success, and our institutions have made repairing individual failure chief among their enterprises.

The evidences of a "therapeutic culture" are being noticed by many thinkers and critics today. In this book I argue that therapy is first and foremost a rhetorical phenomenon. By studying the therapeutic rationale of discourse, I hope to indicate how the rhetoric of this culture proceeds by identifying and resolving our senses of failure, and how failure has become a normal way of doing the business of rhetoric.

ACKNOWLEDGMENTS

Many people deserve thanks for their help in producing the book and the ideas it contains. I thank my wife, Elizabeth Bell, and daughters Miranda and Meredith for giving me life and joy apart from the book and its subject.

Timothy Steckline deserves thanks for good talk about these ideas long ago. Professors Bruce Gronbeck and Donald G. Marshall provided the initial encouragement and direction for putting these ideas into prose. Professor Roderick P. Hart encouraged me to publish these ideas as a book. Professor Robert W. Hopper encouraged me to explore these ideas beyond the present book. Series editor Carroll C. Arnold deserves praise and credit for devoting his time, skills, and thinking to make it a better book.

I wish to thank Professors Richard P. Gregg and Thomas W. Benson, and Professor-to-be Nancy Roth for comments and suggestions about the manuscript.

COPING WITH FAILURE

FAILURE AND RHETORIC

"Failure!" cried William James, "then Failure! so the world stamps us at every turn. We strew it with our blunders, our misdeeds, our lost opportunities, with all the memorials of our inadequacy to our vocation. And with what a damning emphasis does it then blot us out! . . . every pound of flesh exacted is soaked with all its blood."[1] James featured failure in his famous analysis of the "saving" experiences people seek in religious activity. James himself suffered from a psychological sense of failure, a kind of depression then diagnosed as "neurasthenia." As a philosopher and pioneer psychologist he tried to penetrate the ways in which we interpret the general condition of failure and its meanings. He saw that those interpretations are importantly related to the ways we interpret and respond to the world in general.

James understood that the "varieties of religious experience" were one and all attempts to reconcile or repair senses of personal error or inadequacy. He believed that failure motivates the search for ways of transcendence and repair in self and world, a search that is in some form common to all persons. James believed that failures "are pivotal human experiences," and he concluded that "a process so ubiquitous and everlasting is evidently an integral part of life."[2]

People seem almost universally to recognize that failure is part of what it means to be human. We fail because we have not and cannot achieve some ideal that we imagine. We fail because others will not agree to our terms for success. We fail because others, and the world, do not conform to our ideas and ideals and thus disappoint us from the success or status we seek.

When we sense that we have failed, or when failure is thrust upon us, we must repair our confidence if we are to move on—to try again or to shift directions in pursuit of success and satisfaction. This sense of having failed or fallen short of our mark is a *symbolically* constructed sense; failure is an interpretation that is collaborated between self and others about our characters and our situations. To repair or resolve senses of failure, we must induce change in those symbolic collaborations. To induce such changes in someone, either in ourselves or others, is the purpose of rhetoric we make. This book is an inquiry into what we do rhetorically when we collaborate about failure and when as individuals and society we cope with the senses of inadequacy that result.

Religion, as James noticed, is wholly devoted to explaining and reconciling failure. Centuries of drama have been devoted to the subject of failure and its consequences. Psychology and psychiatry, and the entire tradition of therapy, are based upon the need to explain and treat failure. Failure is one of the chief themes of literature and philosophy, and failure is central to the rhetorics of politics and socialization. Even though failure is a prominent theme in virtually every variety of our talk, it is difficult for us to assess the meaning and importance of failure to our lives. We may understand that failure is necessary to change and growth, or that it is our unavoidable fate; yet when we sense personal failure or undergo social failure, feelings of loss and inadequacy are inevitable. Failure demands that we employ our resources to alter, mitigate, or in some way accommodate our sense that self and world have changed.

My central conclusion is that failure evokes a particular kind of thought and expression basic to a form of rhetoric that responds to and is a familiar part of human experience. There is little we say that is not in some degree relevant to the facts of our failures and the possibilities of our failing. Much of what we say reflects our personal and social histories of failure. Or our talk may be meaningful because of potential failures in the present and future. The facts of past inadequacies and the prospects of future failure become, as James apparently believed, a persistent context for discovering meanings and adopting purposes.

People fail because they have plans and goals, and invest themselves in projects to attain their goals. If people did not do things, try to act upon their worlds, if they did not propose to actualize inner wishes and dreams, there could be no senses of inadequacy, misfortune, or error. There could not be failures unless vicissitudes preclude something that is "better": a better result, a goal achieved, an ideal realized. Were it not for people's beliefs that they are important and have the potential to exert their wills in the world, "missing the mark" could not mean that they have failed. But, given such ambitions, all misfortunes and mistakes can be interpreted as failures. Each mishap, regardless of its cause, can be interpreted to mean the failure of some human effort. It is from the idea that we can and should succeed that failure is born.

To appreciate the content and function of rhetoric associated with failure, we must understand the human perspective out of which our rhetorical acts arise and to which they are addressed. The early rhetorical theorist and humanist Protagoras offered a clue in his doctrine of "man the measure of all things." Protagoras can also be read to mean that man is the "measure*r* of all things."[3] People, Protagoras believed, "measure" with their talk, and in that talk they reflect their interpretations of themselves and the world. They measure themselves and their world against "reality"; they measure reality against their ideals; they measure reality and ideals against illusions about what should have been and what might be. In the measuring that is done with talk, the possibilities of error, of falling short, are inevitable parts of the human scale. The consequence is that the judgment of failure involves a circular move. The world is conceived as allowing (and often demanding) failure. Individual shortcomings are then taken as evidence that the world and people are capable of (and often fated to) failure; "failure" is therefore an agreeable interpretation of particular circumstances because it affirms our basic theories of character and human events. There are symbolic remedies for failure at our disposal; to define self or circumstances as failure makes those remedies available means of coping.

The circularity of failure ensures that some fault can be found even for circumstances beyond our control. Wherever fault lies, it can ultimately be judged that a *person* has failed. Even errors that are unavoidable because of lack of knowledge do not excuse us, for they reaffirm human inadequacy and imperfection. It would seem that greater knowledge and understanding would allow people to go beyond these simplistic means of coping with hardship. But, as Ecclesiastes says, "In much wisdom is much vexation, and he who increases knowledge increases sorrow." Greater knowledge often brings about greater awareness of fault, keener awareness of shortcoming, and more acute senses of inadequacy. Each new awareness of conditions opens up new possibilities for failing, new kinds of possible "faults," new targets for "blame," and often a new language by which failure, fault, and blame may be expressed.

In this book I wish to explore how judgments of failure are formed, why they are appealing and sometimes useful interpretations for managing human experience. Failure is a symbolic way of accounting for personal and social events; it helps us to sort out possibilities and options, and it interprets experience in ways that direct us to solutions. This procedure, of course, can be both beneficial and harmful. Either way, the sorting through and reformulation of experience is done by means of interpretation, and through the means of persuasion at our disposal.

Responsiveness to the world and responsibility for the world require definitions of failure. Within the perimeters of those definitions a person

5

must persuade self and perhaps others that *this* interpretation of failure is "true" and *that* course of response is "better" than alternative courses. In such cases, we attempt to induce changes via symbolic behavior, and by definition this symbolic action is *rhetorical.*

The presence of failure implies a world where rhetorical thought and expression are important—at times, paramount. To fail, to experience failure, or to be a failure requires that one accept a definition of the world and self wherein failure is a possibility. With such a definition accepted, we can ascribe to failure the quality of a threat, warn against it as a likelihood, or invoke it as a condition of life, human fate, or a natural law. As Ch. Perelman and L. Olbrechts-Tyteca have stressed, the "definitions" we compose or embrace are "arguments" about the way the world is.[4] Definitions claim to have gotten things "right." Definitions are rhetorical standards, and standards of failure define what is right and what is mistaken. When we ask what human suffering, misery, crisis, loss, humiliation, disappointment, anger, anxiety, loneliness, and despair *mean,* it is possible to answer by saying that someone or something has "failed." The very declaration that someone is or was inadequate or mistaken implicitly argues rhetorically.

William James grasped the important fact that our understandings of failure are integral to our interpretations of what living means. James wrote that "our nature being thus rooted in failure, is it any wonder that theologians should have held it essential, and thought that only through the personal experience of humiliation which it engenders the deeper sense of life's significance is reached?"[5] In *Fallible Man,* Paul Ricoeur notices that failure is the defining characteristic of the Christian view of man. In *The Symbolism of Evil* Ricoeur examines the way that we transform our ontological fallibility into "fault" by using the symbolic resources of "evil."[6] Ricoeur shows us how an entire world view can rest upon one overarching interpretation of failure and its meaning—its causes and consequences. An interpretation of the world that posits the universal presence of "evil" asserts one meaning for human life and action. Living and acting are fundamentally executions of or avoidances of *evil.* Evil then gets combined with interpretations of human character; we have meaningful identities because our characters are receptive to, and potential sources of, evil.

Mircea Eliade has also observed that Christianity is "the religion of 'fallen man.' "[7] "Fallen man" and "fallible man" are interpretations that support the basic rhetorical functions of religious explanation. To explain and treat failure requires some general theory or doctrine that accounts for and interprets losses in humanly meaningful terms. That is why in religions, human failure and human suffering are the given conditions of life. Eliade writes that "in each case the suffering becomes intelligible and hence tolerable." We "struggle" against our "suffering," Eliade says, "with all the magico-religious means available," but are able to tolerate suffering "morally because *it is not absurd.*"[8]

As Eliade suggests, we muster our symbolic resources to fight against failure, forming general explanations and techniques of response, whether those be magical, religious, or scientific. But the motives of explanation and treatment come into conflict in our usual ways of responding. Explanations require that failure is the norm to be expected. Such explanations diminish our character as beings. Yet treatment requires a view that failure can be overcome, that people are significant. The same possibility of failure that guarantees our humility also provides our self-importance. This bind is illustrated in the contemporary therapy drama *Ordinary People*. There a boy and his therapist struggle to redefine the failure the boy feels because he was unable to save his brother from drowning. The therapist insists to the boy that he was not responsible, that the failure was not his. The boy replies, "You don't understand, it has to be somebody's fault, or what was the whole point of it?" The boy confronts a familiar choice between two failures: either accept that your actions are meaningless and incapable of fighting random misfortune, or accept that you personally failed to act and are personally responsible. The boy's dilemma is not unlike that of Hamlet. He must choose a tortured existence or choose not to exist at all. As with Hamlet, there are powerful human reasons why the boy in *Ordinary People* must cling to his guilt.

Dwight Conquergood tells the story of how his Laotian pupils became frustrated when there was to be an eclipse of the moon. In Laotian culture a lunar eclipse is interpreted as "frog-eat-moon." The "cosmic frog" eats the moon when people have been at some fault. When the eclipse occurs, the people must frighten the frog by banging sticks and pans and making whatever noise they can, prompting the frog to regurgitate the moon. The Laotians in Chicago were eager to assimilate Western knowledge of eclipses, but they were confused, saying, "Teacher, we do not know how to *do* 'eclipse.'" Heretofore eclipses had been caused by their failures, and these failures were somehow righted by *doing* symbolic responses. Now their new understanding of the Western view of eclipses told them their actions had nothing to do with producing or ending eclipses. The Laotian tradition gave importance to people and their participation in the world because they could fail and could generate "eclipse." The Western world view asserts that people have "nothing

7

to do" with such affairs. Westerners might believe that new scientific knowledge would relieve the Laotians of their irrational burden of failure, but it is more likely that this knowledge closes off avenues of participation in the world and is potentially humiliating to their senses of self-importance.

The Laotians' folklore illustrates what appears to be a normal human tendency to interpret the world with the expectation that our actions influence it. Even within the scientific world view, Westerners exhibit drives to "harness" tides, to "control" climate, to "hybridize" plant and animal life. Indeed, much of scientific rhetoric is devoted to defining, interpreting, and choosing remedial actions to repair faults in our relationships to nature. With every new scientific study about the ecological effects of our society, it seems we are burdened with new failures and new guilt for our actions. Westerners *do* eclipse in scientific and popular ways of observing the event. Such practices are among the ways we express awe, valor, pride, and humility in our relationship with nature.

The Laotians' tradition and much scientific rhetoric are instances of seemingly universal impulses to symbolize human mastery of the world. It was achievement of this mastery that Protagoras saw in our rhetorical ways of measuring reality. The scientific view, as does the Laotian practice, illustrates the fact that our failures and inadequacies are intimately bound up with our motivations for achievement and participation in the world. As the philosopher Henry W. Johnstone, Jr., has said, "In a society of perfect men, rhetoric would not be needed."[9] Without failure there would be no need for change in our knowledge, evaluations, actions, or ways of ordering the world.

When an individual defines himself or herself as a failure, he or she does so to manage a situation in a particular way. When an individual or group has been judged a failure, or to be in danger of failing, the only response possible is a rhetorical one. Any response must affirm, redefine, or reinterpret the failure. One can deny that the failure exists, or affirm or deny that it has the qualities and degrees of "fault" or "blame" others have given it. Any judgment of failure as a fact, accusation, or even as a latent possibility creates a situation that is rhetorical because it asserts and demands a rhetorical response. A moment's reflection will make one realize how vast a number of human situations and rhetorical responses to them involve creating and trying to resolve issues of failure.

Failure is, however, more than a fact or possibility to be discussed. Failure is also a concept—an abstract, general, and qualitative notion. It is a concept that allows us to generalize from individual experiences to broader conceptions about situations and their causes and consequences.

From an individual experience of failure one is invited to generalize about the meaning of one's life, or life itself. "Failure" assigns a basic "faulty" character to people and experiences, even though there may be numerous ideas of cause, meaning, and consequences in any given case. To interpret an event or experience as "failure" is to employ a concept with great rhetorical fecundity, and it is that fecundity that I propose to explore in the following pages.

A sense of failure motivates rhetorical responses that imply further responses aimed at resolving the failure and its attendant problems. The power of failure to motivate resolving responses is so great that we often invoke failure as an interpretation precisely to bring about the kinds of attitudes and actions that are associated with it. Our resolutions may be pragmatic or spiritual, involving the policies of a politician, promotion in business, religious beliefs, rearing children, self-renewal and reform of character, or proposals for solving difficulties brought on by having located and identified a "failure" in persons or the world.

Failure is an interpretation of experience that creates and shapes our rhetorical ways of coping. Failure is part of the fabric of our identities as individuals or groups or even as humans. When we identify and locate fault and blame, when we define and interpret failure, individual selves are almost inevitably involved. Our repairs for failures involve human, personal responses that must be made. It is therefore necessary to consider the relations of failure and the self, the relations between failure and our rhetorical projects to manage identity.

NOTES

1. William James, *The Varieties of Religious Experience* (New York: Modern Library, 1929), 135.

2. James, 135.

3. See Mario Untersteiner's interpretation of Protagoras' statement as man the "master" of all things: *The Sophists,* trans. Kathleen Freeman (New York: Philosophical Library, 1954), esp. p. 53.

4. Ch. Perelman and L. Olbrechts-Tyteca, *The New Rhetoric: A Treatise on Argumentation* (Notre Dame, IN: University of Notre Dame Press, 1969), 213.

5. James, 138.

6. Paul Ricoeur, *Fallible Man: Philosophy of the Will,* trans. Charles Kelbley (Chicago: Regnery, 1965); *The Symbolism of Evil,* trans. Emerson Buchanan (New York: Harper, 1967).

7. Mircea Eliade, *The Myth of the Eternal Return,* trans. Willard R. Trask (New York: Pantheon, 1954), 162.

8. Eliade, 97–99.

9. Henry W. Johnstone, Jr., in *The Prospect for Rhetoric,* eds. Lloyd Bitzer and Edwin Black (Englewood Cliffs, NJ: Prentice-Hall, 1971), 83.

2

FAILURE AND PERSONAL IDENTITY

What are the rhetorical activities of "self" and how does failure figure into them? A young and frustrated Kenneth Burke asked the question in this way: "How is it that one may transform his failures into profit, not in the sense of those who leave failure behind them . . . but in the sense of those whose structure of existence is made of the materials of their frustration?"[1] Burke and James worked through their personal senses of failure in philosophy and theory, forging perspectives on "the structure of existence" that allowed them to suffer their personal pains with at least tolerance and understanding. Others seek out structures of existence within the doctrines and causes of religions, mass movements, political parties, psychotherapy, the business world and careers. Education, primary socialization, and typical value orientations also provide us with such structures as help us use failures to secure our identities and successes. How failure figures in the motivation for our involvements and commitments is a central consideration in this book.

When people analyze and respond to failure, they have their "selves" and what is today called their "identities" as their chief frames of reference. The character and continuity of our selves are plotted in personal narratives that seem to revolve around our failures. This is perhaps what James meant when he said that failures are "pivotal human experiences." In the dramatism of personal life, failure is connected with the "fate," "salvation," or "success" of the self. In our literature and lore failure is the prelude to "growth," "renewal," and eventual success.

Burke alluded to the rhetorical option of dealing with failure by transforming it into profit. While failure can have tragic consequences, people usually attempt to define and interpret failure so that some pattern of success will emerge. One may interpret failure so that one derives a changed or improved self. This can be achieved by identifying with something larger and grander than oneself, as in a religion or a mass movement. There are also rhetorics today that so enlarge and aggrandize self that the same effect is had through devotion to self and its formation.

11

Whatever the particulars of the rhetoric, there is reason to believe that the transformation of self from a failed condition to one that offers success is central to the motivation. This is what Eric Hoffer tried to establish in *The True Believer*. In Hoffer's analysis it is the individual's sense of inadequacy or frustration that brings him or her to seek out the offerings of a "cause"—even though the cause of the crusade or movement is cast in the rhetoric of collective, spiritual, and eternal purification. The rhetoric of a movement supplies theories and diagnoses of what has led to the individual's sense of failure. The flaw may be doctrinally defined as sin, bourgeoisie ideology, secular humanism, or some other. Each such diagnosis implies a certain kind of identity that embodies the fault; each prescription for belief and action implies the kind of identity that is free of this fault.

It is not difficult to see that the rhetoric of a cause or movement offers curative procedures for the faults and failures individuals experience. Within the frameworks of their analyses, movements prescribe social roles and identify actions to achieve those roles. Movements offer rhetorical models, case analyses, persuasive training, and rhetorical opportunities to persuade an audience with the newly learned rhetoric. In these ways collectives sustain faith and give purpose to the actions of individuals who, as Hoffer put it, seek to "dissolve their spoiled, meaningless selves in some soul-stirring, communal undertaking."[2]

Hoffer's analysis of how the rhetoric of collectivity speaks to the rhetorical needs of individual selves runs against a common belief about mass movements. At least since Gustave LeBon promulgated the idea of a "crowd mind" in 1895, there has been a pervasive tendency to attribute a kind of magical power to the rhetoric of mass movements. Many times theorists of social change seem to accept the mystical claims a movement makes about collective action and being, and seek to understand the collective psychology that mass action presumes to engender. Hoffer attempted to separate the phenomenon of mass behavior from the rhetorical accounts of why the "mass" is so powerful.

A focus on the rhetorical uses of failure suggests that the ultimate proofs of the claims of any movement lie in the usefulness of the claims to an individual's project of self-persuasion. Whether a movement is a religious crusade or a political cause, or even one of the cults of herbal remedies, real estate entrepreneurs, or self-help healers on late-night television, the central speakers testify to some previous failure and give personal accounts of their recovery via the doctrine, life style, or product they are trying to sell. These rhetorical appeals communicate techniques of resolving failure that are useful to audiences who also must deal with their personal inadequacies. Rhetoric generally appeals by offering individuals symbols that resolve conflicts and pressures and by providing instructions for their application, a great deal of which is accomplished in the individual interactions that accompany a movement or cause.

At least in American society, public persuasion often focuses on individual identity as the source of problems and on changing individual identity as the key to solving those problems. Such rhetoric implicitly and explicitly ties a broad range of personal and public failures to perceived flaws in individual identity, prescribing improved identities that remedy failure and avoid failure in the future. "Identity" is an operational construct of the rhetoric and identity change becomes a rhetorical means to achieve diverse persuasive ends. In this rhetoric we can observe the relationship of failure to projects of self-change.

An interesting comparison and contrast of recent "identity rhetorics" can be had from two recent books, *The Aquarian Conspiracy* and *In Search of Excellence*.[3] These books possess vastly divergent purposes and visions of the present age. Furthermore, neither book offers the doctrine of an existing movement. Each attempts in some way to construct a collective sense of purpose by addressing its readers as individuals, and by using individual identity as the basis for collective action.

In her appeal to the "new Aquarians," Marilyn Ferguson argues that a "conspiracy of individuals" exists and is collaborating on some mysterious level, and that the result of this conspiracy will be a new breakthrough in human self-awareness and spiritual discovery. Corporate consultants Thomas J. Peters and Robert H. Waterman, Jr., appeal to entrepreneurs and corporate managers to join in a quest for "excellence" in the corporate marketplace. They believe that the shared values and techniques of seeking excellence will improve the roles and identities of individuals in companies and companies in society, and improve consumerism in general. Politically and ideologically these two theses are as far apart as seems possible. Ferguson bolsters the spiritual faith of the "old" counterculture. Peters and Waterman shape a "new" ethic of success for the business community.

What the rhetorics of the two books share is a focus on individual identity as the means of accomplishing the goal. In the views of these authors individuals must be capable of change in order to attain either spiritual growth or material success. Individuals must change themselves if they are to participate in either the "conspiracy" or "corporation" of individuals. Rhetorically, the possibility of self-change must be rendered legitimate and techniques of implementing self-change must be supplied. The role of failure in these rhetorical operations is clear.

13

Consider the kinds of failure the audiences for these books are likely to have experienced. In the late 1970s and early 1980s, the Aquarian ideology of self-awareness and self-discovery suffered from obscurity, trivialization, and political failure. The "new conservatism" threatened the Aquarian vision of a future peopled by spiritual seekers. At least part of this new conservatism was a response to a decade of "diminished expectations," where business prospects had seemed to suffer, the material future seemed bleak, and public interest in and governmental support for corporate ideology had waned.

The Aquarian Conspiracy and *In Search of Excellence* address these perceived failures as failures of *attitude*. They are both instances of "inspirational" rhetoric, seeking to rehabilitate the central values of their respective ideologies. Failure to achieve either the spiritual goals of "consciousness" or the material goals of "success" is, in the final analysis, a rhetorical failure to motivate individuals to change. This can be accomplished, however, by explaining individuals' failures for them and offering them success in and through participation in "Aquarian" or "excellence" ideology.

Both books expend much effort establishing that the individual is the most important "value" of their respective causes. Whether one sets out to people the world with seekers or with properly oriented employees and consumers, one's success depends on individuals' valuing themselves in special ways and being willing to change the failing attitudes that dominate them. Thus the general or collective diagnosis of failure establishes identification between the purposes of the books and the individuals who sense individual failure. This identification established, a technique of change must be offered and be justified as a legitimate way of solving the problem.

The two books handle the problem of how to attain the needed changes in interestingly paradoxical ways. To legitimize spiritual "psychotechnologies" of personal transformation, Ferguson resorts to a theory of physical and material transformation. The managerial materialists, however, tie their legitimation strategies to a theory of personal, spiritual actualization. Ferguson asserts that psychological transformation is a response to a universal necessity—a "law" of change that applies to both material and humanistic experience:

"We are at a very exciting moment in history, perhaps a turning point," said Ilya Prigogine, who won the 1977 Nobel Prize for a theory that describes transformations, not only in the physical sci-

14

ences but also in society—the role of stress and "perturbations" that can thrust us into a new, higher order.

Science, he said, is proving the reality of a "deep cultural vision." The poets and philosophers were right in their intimations of an open, creative universe. Transformation, innovation, evolution—these are the natural responses to crisis.[4]

The legitimizing move here is simple: to the extent that you perceive these as times of crisis, a natural law can explain this to you as a stage in deep cultural transformation that makes it only natural that you, too, will be and should be transformed. You should be ready to change as part of this massive progression. Ferguson continues: "The crises of our times, it becomes increasingly clear, are the impetus for revolution now underway. And once we understand nature's transformative powers, we see that it is our powerful ally, not a force to be feared or subdued. *Our pathology is our opportunity.*"[5] The reader now knows the source of the "failure" and the direction of remedial action. Further, this spiritual direction is both materially and scientifically legitimate, and inevitable.

The prophets of excellence also must legitimize their techniques for transforming corporate images. To do so, they also need a theory of failure. Rather than going to the physical universe for their principle of failure, these authors go to a psychological theory. They appropriate Ernest Becker's theory of "death" motivation to posit one basic cause of failure in corporate motivation: the individual "needs at one and the same time to be a conforming member of a winning team and to be a star in his own right." They continue:

About the winning team, Becker notes: "society . . . is a vehicle for earthly heroism. . . . Man transcends death by finding meaning for his life. . . . It is the burning desire for the creature to count. . . . What man really fears is not so much extinction, but extinction with *insignificance.* . . . Ritual is the technique for giving life. His sense of self worth is constituted symbolically, his cherished narcissism feeds on symbols, on an abstract idea of his own worth. [Man's] natural yearning can be fed limitlessly in the domain of symbols." He adds: "*Men fashion unfreedom* [a large measure of conformity] *as a bribe for self-perpetuation.*" In other words, men willingly shackle themselves to the nine-to-five only if the cause is perceived to be in some sense great. The company can actually provide the same resonance as does the exclusive club or honorary society.[6]

15

It is doubtful that either Prigogine or Becker would be very supportive of the causes toward which their theories are here applied. However, Ferguson and Peters and Waterman felt the need to ground their techniques in a sweeping theory of failure. Both drew from their respective theories: (1) an explanation of individual failure that (2) associated this failure with some value that needs to be filled, and (3) legitimized the techniques to be used in filling the need and actualizing the value. If crises bring about transformation, then one should seek out the "psychotechnologies" of personal transformation; if people need symbols of individuality and achievement, then give them those symbols through the resources of your company and its successful identity.

This rhetoric, like other motivational rhetoric today, isolates individual identity as the locus of both the cause of, and solution for failure. It is in the failure of individual selves that the problems are manifest, and it is by address to and change of selves that even those problems beyond individual identities can be solved. The rhetoric offers each individual the opportunity to see his or her personal failings as due to a single cause and as being of one substance, either as parts of some momentous perturbation in the cosmos or as manifestations of the universal need for humans to find significance in the face of death. Our failures being so charged with ideological significance, the solutions will be also.

In making her case for the Aquarian Conspiracy, Ferguson makes a number of accurate observations about contemporary rhetoric and social change. She notes that identity is today treated as the medium of social change, and that public appeals today "emphasize attitude, not behavior."[7] This is a fair characterization of more rhetoric than the psychic lore that informs her own. It is standard for speakers to argue that something is wrong, that actions and choices have led to difficulty, but the contemporary move is to locate the causes of those problems in our individual identities—in our attitudes, beliefs, and values. Out of these psychologistical problems unfortunate actions and choices are born. The problems are not then to be solved by changes of policy or by collective efforts alone; there must first be changes of individual attitudes, beliefs, and values. The rhetorical means of accomplishing this is to form new identities. This is a widely used pattern of motivational rhetoric.

Indeed, the rhetorical pattern of "success" consultants Peters and Waterman is very similar to that of the "Reagan revolution." The themes of excellence and being a winner echo in both, as does the idea that a winning collective identity is based upon resolving individual failures. Reagan's focus on national character as the cause of our moral and economic shortcomings was not unlike the consultants' focus on corporate identity. Reagan's remedy for problems of national identity was to appeal for loyalty and commitment to the "company" in order to form a national identity in which the best expressions of individual success could occur. National character would not shape individual character, but individual character would, as it were, reshape the national character. Exactly as the nucleus of Peters and Waterman's management theory specifies, Reagan sought solutions based upon individual identification with shared values that either a corporation or nation can embody in its image.[8]

A rhetorical approach more akin to Ferguson's spiritual "conspiracy" appeared in Jimmy Carter's 1976 presidential campaign. Carter claimed in the post–Watergate period that our fault lay in lack of moral excellence. He stated to more than one campaign crowd:

> Our country is made up of pluralism, diversity. A lot of different kinds of people. But that's not a sign of weakness, it's a sign of strength. Some people have said that our nation is a melting pot. It's not. Whether we came to this country two years, twenty years, two hundred years ago—it doesn't matter. The point is why we came to this country. But when we come here, we haven't given up our individuality, our pride in our past history or background or commitments or habits. We become not a melting pot, but a beautiful mosaic. Different people, different beliefs, different yearnings, different hopes, different dreams.[9]

The sociology of Carter's following had something to do with his appeals to pluralism and ethnicity, but the idea of "individuality" provided him with a basis for uniting minorities with other believers, some of whom were Ferguson's "Aquarians."

Most Democratic candidates promote some image of collectivity, such as the melting pot, the New Frontier, or the Great Society. It is interesting that in 1976 Carter thought it desirable to provide a collective image that preserved and gave praise to the individualities and the inner dreams of his audience. The "dream" had become a collective symbol of the protest movement, yet Carter addressed the pluralism of that movement as a collection of individual, inner dreams.

The idea of "inner" motivation is patent in therapeutic self-help literature. Motivation must come from inside, for it is ultimately the individual who must undertake to improve the self. Ferguson claims that this thrust represents a change in rhetorical habits. She says, "Individuals are beginning to sustain social concern and action in ways never accomplished by outer influences." She lists those "outer" influences as "persuasion, propaganda, patriotism, religious injunction, threats, preachments of brotherhood."[10] Public rhetoric in America has traditionally invited respondents to seek higher identification through commitments to causes outside themselves. This was true of the mass movements Hoffer studied. By contrast, Ferguson sees individual and inner values as spiritually prior to collective values, and Carter saw them as at least rhetorically or pragmatically prior for his audience.

At least since 1976, when Tom Wolfe coined the phrase "the 'me' decade," popular discourse has placed striking emphasis on the success and well-being of individuals—as measured in individual fulfillment and "effectiveness" of personality.[11] Others have bemoaned the "fall of public man," and pronounced ours a "culture of narcissism."[12] Of course, emphasis on individualism and personality has been in steady evolution in Western society, and has been traced through developments in ancient Greece, Christianity, Kant, Hegel, Machiavelli, the Italian Renaissance, and Victorian England.[13] Whatever the history of this emphasis, it is widely accepted in America today that happiness and success for individuals derive from "right" self-perception and from "right" attitudes, those that most effectively serve the individual. What seems to me significant is that there is a self-conscious, rhetorical focus on individual identity as the spring by which personal achievement and public weal are powered. Further, achievement and execution of individual identity can be reduced to a set of personal, rhetorical strategies that bring about both personal and social well-being. This is not the only fountainhead of rhetoric in our times, but the ability and need for change of individual identity is a common assumption among contemporary audiences and rhetors. So much so that some contemporary sociological researchers have wondered if middle-class Americans are "trapped in a therapeutic rhetoric," and worry that they may become incapable of expressing social commitment.[14] The ideas that individuals are responsible for their identities and that the world should be responsive to their identities are important pragmatic facts about rhetoric today.

RHETORICAL THEORIES OF SELF

Rhetoric that aims at improving life through perfecting identities presupposes three things. First, such rhetoric is devised on the assumption that identity or the self is changeable and changing. Conceptions of how and why identities change are theoretically vital to any such rhetorical operations. Second, this rhetoric implies a belief that identity is formed,

18

sustained, and reformed through communication—through symbolic exchange. This is implied in any interactive view of identity formation and change. Third, and in consequence of the second assumption, it is assumed that people can be persuaded to change their orientations and actions by changing their identities, and that the results will be gratifying and uplifting for selves and society.

William Barrett has observed that we live in an age of technique, where we share the "illusion" that human problems will be met with the applied knowledge of social science.[15] Contemporary psychological, sociological, and social-psychological theories undergird the techniques of therapeutic rhetoric, supplying persuaders and audiences with conceptions and vocabularies of identity change. In these conceptions and vocabularies we can observe the psychological assumptions available to contemporary persuaders. Current theories of identity are essentially rhetorical theories of self.

The psychologist Roy F. Baumeister reviewed historical and current theories of identity and concluded that "to a psychologist, identity seems to be something that exists within the personality or a set of cognitions. . . . In this [sociologists'] view identity is a set of roles and statuses, arranged by how they are defined by society."[16] Baumeister echoes an important contemporary conclusion, that identity must be psychosocial. That is, whatever an individual's identity is, it must somehow be both part and product of the interaction between self and society. Identity is then a *symbol,* one that mediates between personality and social role.

Baumeister believes that a "context for identity" must be conceived as having both psychological and sociological dimensions and that we must address the "functional aspects of identity." This means that any individual's personal context for assessing identity must answer questions about the self for the self. Baumeister lists these questions as: "How shall I relate to others? What shall I strive to become? How will I make the basic decisions needed to guide life?" In this functional sense, Baumeister believes, identity "can be understood as a theory about the self."[17] As a "theory," an individual's identity is open to persuasion and change. In a significant respect it must be the product of previous persuasive experiences with self and others. Also, one's theory of self must be strongly informed and influenced by prevailing theories of identity that abound in contemporary rhetoric.

Failure or its possibility is often the context in which the self must devise answers to Baumeister's three questions. Indeed, failure must be both psychological and sociological, involving social expressions of personal failure and personal experiences of social failure. Like any other theory, one's theory of self must be revised when it fails to explain the data of experience.

Were it not for the demands of psychic and social life, one would never need to answer Baumeister's basic questions about self. Were there never failure to relate to others (and never a theory that formulated the problem thus), there would be no uncertainty about how one's identity functions to perform relations. Were there no rhetoric that suggested that one could be something other than one is, or that one should become something better than one is, there would be no need to ask and answer "How shall I strive to be?" Were there no decisions to be made about guiding one's life, there would be no need for religious doctrines, theories of self or identity, ethics, or processes of social modeling.

Baumeister suggests the rhetorical nature of identity when he concludes that "identity is a definition, an interpretation of self."[18] He agrees that people have always had something we could call "identities," but he believes that there is something distinctive about the current widespread and sophisticated use of the concept. Baumeister suggests that "the modern difficulty with identity must be understood as resulting from a change in identity, or rather the way that identity is created and shaped."[19] However, neither he nor his colleagues in psychology or sociology recognize explicitly that the processes of definition and interpretation, and of creating, shaping, and changing such definitions and interpretations, are *rhetorical* activities. These processes involve symbolic formulations that are persuasive to those who formulate and express them to others.

Although their focus has not often been rhetorical, symbolic-interactionist perspectives such as Baumeister's tend to recognize that "identity" is the product of communication between self and society. Yet seldom have we noticed how important events of failure are to observing this fact. Theorists continually examine instances of self-social misalignment precisely to discover, as does Baumeister, that interaction between self and society functions to realign and reintegrate individual psyches with social roles.

The work of Erving Goffman is a compendium on embarrassment and failure. He focused on the self's strategies to manage conflict and tension between personal/psychological reality and social norms and expectations. This focus led Goffman to study events of failure, institutions that harbor social failures, and how communication is used to construct and manage "stigma."[20] In his notes on adaptation to failure, Goffman offered a highly rhetorical account of how individuals and society manage failures of identity. He wrote of an "art of consolation" whereby there is achieved "a sort of social sanitation enjoining torn and tattered persons to keep themselves packaged up."[21] To Goffman, a failure was a person who "can no longer sustain one of his social roles and is about to be removed from it; he is a person who is losing one of his social lives and is about to die one of the deaths possible for him."[22] The "art of consolation" is a set of communicative strategies that facilitate a kind of acquiescence to this death, or possibly engender some form of "rebirth" for the failed individual.

Goffman saw an individual's identity as an integration of "his several life activities." As a symbol or theory, identity serves to integrate oneself across the various pressures, roles, and situations in which an individual must function. What he found remarkable was that individuals can, through the art of consolation, "sustain such profound embarrassments," and be divided and reunified through the appropriate kinds of communicative actions.[23] Goffman's analysis suggests that one's "integrity" can be destroyed by failure and repaired by communicative strategies that integrate the various elements of one's identity.

Another particularly interesting treatment of psychosocial identity is that of Erik Erikson. Erikson has explored the concept of identity crisis and the identity changes that take place throughout stages of life. His theory is reflected in Baumeister's conclusion that there are psychological and social elements of identity that are necessary to the function of that identity for the individual.[24]

Erikson writes that there are three "complementarities" on which the study of psychosocial identity depends: "the personal coherence of the individual and role integration in his group; his guiding images and the ideologies of his time; his life history—and the historical moment."[25] These seem to be precisely the psychological factors that Eric Hoffer implicitly identified as motives for adopting the rhetoric of a mass movement. Erikson suggests that these three pairings may be only different aspects of one essential "complementarity," the relationship of self to society.

I believe Erikson has come upon three dialectical pairs that characterize dialogue between self and society. Erikson's pairs indicate that there are three important avenues of self-definition and self-change. In rhetorical terms, these are the basic *topoi* of therapeutic discourse. Private and public talk provides both personal coherence and role integration; talk unifies the "guiding images" of the individual with and through ideology; and talk establishes the continuity between one's life history and the future-tensed "moment" in which we act. Erikson's descriptive categories represent rhetorical *topoi* that I will treat as *self–society, past–future,* and *spiritual–material.* Analysis of how these *topoi* are used to achieve the related goals of self-definition and dealing with failure is the substance of most of what follows in this book.

Berger and Luckmann treat the conceptual pair self–society as a "dialectic" through which social reality is constructed.[26] Rhetorical theorists have made great use of this work, yet have not fully appreciated how much this theory focuses on individual identity and the broadly therapeutic operations of communication. Berger and Luckmann posit that the dialectic of self and society occurs within three continuous "moments" in the interaction of subjective and objective realities. Accordingly, "society" is created by the *externalization* of individual subjective realities. This social reality is "objective" inasmuch as *objectivation* by individual and collective actions gives it an institutional character. The third moment in this dialectic is *internalization,* "by which the objectivated social world is retrojected into consciousness in the course of socialization."[27] Berger and Luckmann see self-change, what they call "alternation," as a necessary and perhaps inevitable part of the social dialectic. Alternation requires that individuals internalize social definitions and actualize them in self-changes as part of the ongoing construction and management of reality. Managing social reality entails dealing through language with the moments where the dialectic does not work perfectly to align self and society. These are conditions that lead to feelings and interpretations of failure. The institutional and language-based processes that arise from these conditions Berger and Luckmann term "therapy." I wish now to discuss that concept from a distinctively rhetorical point of view.

Rhetoricians long ago saw that the processes of socialization were executed in and through rhetoric. Ancient studies of rhetoric categorized and described the symbolic patterns and processes by which humans create social reality and bring that social reality to bear on individual actions and character. One of the systematic patterns they discerned is discourse that addresses character and worth by praising or blaming persons and institutions. In the language of Perelman and Olbrechts-Tyteca, one seeks through this sort of discourse "to establish a sense of communion centered around particular values [already] recognized by the audience."[28] Traditionally this discourse has focused on social values and commitments, but today it often operates in situations where individuality is the chief value shared by a given audience. We saw instances of this kind of epideictic discourse in Carter's speech, in Ferguson's "conspiracy," and in the corporate "identity" designed to foster excellence in its

22

employees and clientele. Whether social or individual values are at stake, epideictic discourse weighs worth. Persuaders construct assessments of self and society around such central themes as Berger and Luckmann describe in their theory. I will detail the moves that are made in these dialectical processes in later chapters. For now, I want to emphasize that there is, in fact, a logic to praise–blame in rhetoric, and that this activity is and always has been concerned with the character and worth of self.

Alasdair MacIntyre expressed the logic according to which psychosocial identity and worth must be interlocked with failure. His description of "pre-philosophical" Greece applies to Western society generally:

> I fail to be *agathos* if and only if I fail to bring off the requisite performances; and the function of expressions of praise and blame is to invoke and to justify the rewards of success and the penalties of failure. You cannot avoid blame and penalty by pointing out that you could not help doing what you did, that failure was unavoidable. You may, of course, certainly point this out; but if your performance failed to satisfy the appropriate criteria, then you simply cannot prevent the withdrawal of the ascription of kingliness, courage, and cleverness or cunning [*agathos*].[29]

Agathos is an evaluative term meaning generally "good," though MacIntyre here indicates its more specific Homeric meanings. He points out that by the time of the great Sophists in ancient Greece this virtue of social performance was more narrowly defined as *aretê,* meaning "excellence," which the Sophists claimed to teach through training in epideictic rhetoric.[30] The Sophists understood the curative value of rhetoric, and this early we can see the development of what I am calling therapeutic rhetoric.

The criteria of success and failure change, and we may today be experiencing a significant change in the relative priorities of individual virtues and social virtues used in praising and blaming. But the socializing function of epideictic and the use of symbols to argue success and failure seem only to undergo changes in form or format. Erving Goffman's "post-philosophical" description of the role of values in constituting individual identity parallels MacIntyre's focus on worth:

> For the purposes of analysis, one may think of an individual in reference to the values or attributes of a socially recognized character which he possesses. Psychologists speak of a value as a personal involvement. Sociologists speak of a value as a status, a role, or relationship. In either case, the character of the value that is pos-

sessed is taken in a certain way as the character of the person who possesses it. An alteration in the kinds of attributes possessed brings an alteration to the self-conception of the person who possesses them.[31]

According to Goffman, an individual makes a public claim about what attributes he or she possesses. This is a distinctively rhetorical view of the self's activities. He continues: "The limits to a person's claims, and hence the limits to his self, are primarily determined by the objective facts of his social life and secondarily by the degree to which a sympathetic interpretation can bend them in his favor."[32] Goffman was primarily concerned with the strategic situation of a self who must manage public identity, hence he does not mention that the "objective facts" of one's life, and their interpretations, are also constantly the subjects of talk, both public and private, in which we praise and blame ourselves for our actions and commitments.

The most significant contemporary treatment of rhetoric and socialization is that of Kenneth Burke. Burke's rhetorical theories incorporate the contemporary symbolic-interactionist views. As early as 1937 Burke formulated a rhetorical description of self–social processes in terms of identity.[33] In his concept of rhetoric as identification, Burke observes how individuals must, through language, manage the alignments and misalignments in dialectical contests between social demands and the purposes of self-survival and ambition.[34] The values and meanings present in our discourse, Burke believes, are sources from which we persuade ourselves about our identities, the substance of which is publicly and privately formed in active identification of self with the values and meanings contained in discourse. The view of rhetoric as curative—i.e., therapeutic—can be traced through the huge corpus of Burke's work.

The theories and perspectives I have reviewed here support basic propositions about rhetoric and its therapeutic functions: (1) Communicative activities relevant to addressing self-identity, self-worth, and the potentials of self involve symbolizing with persuasive purpose and design. These activities seek changes in or seek to stabilize (integrate) symbolic identity and its status. These activities are therefore inherently rhetorical and are an important pretext of public and private discourse. (2) The possibility of failure is an important thematic and structural element in these communicative activities. Recognition and characterization of failure is a typical way of initiating and/or executing the therapeutic functions of communication. (3) Public or private efforts to define, change, or stabilize identity employ the rhetorical resources of traditional social lore and practices and incorporate theoretical and technical conceptions of identity and self-change made available in public talk and expression. (4) Rhetorical analysis of the symbolic efforts we expend in these directions can enrich understanding of identity and social forces or structures. A rhetorical analysis of these efforts can show the formal and functional properties of a wide range of rhetoric. (5) To isolate the properties and functions of discourse that deals with failure, the term "therapeutic rhetoric" is useful. By this term I seek to indicate curative uses and functions of rhetorical action for selves who seek out persuasion or seek to persuade self and others. As I have argued, these uses and functions are traditional to rhetorical study, but they have not been a predominant focus of contemporary rhetorical or psychological perspectives.

THERAPEUTIC PERSUASION

The self exists in a context where the possibilities of failure are prominent. To a great degree, the motives and strategies of persuasion are those associated with self-maintenance and self-change. Kenneth Burke's theories of communication as "symbolic action" focus analysis directly on these aspects of rhetorical activity. His studies of language and social structure examine the way symbols are themselves constructed and used in psychological and social contexts. Burke stresses the interactive and cooperative participation of speaker and audience in the enactment of persuasion, through which and from which individuals draw symbolic sustenance. The special strength of his analyses has been to show how these therapeutic processes are executed in the rationale of the discourse itself.

Burke's analyses advance the important principle that the needs or situations of a speaker and an audience may not be identical, but may both achieve integration by participating in the same message or symbolic act. Integration or service to their separate selves is achieved through cooperative techniques for symbolizing, defining, and interpreting themselves—techniques that are made available in rhetoric.

Burke illustrated this possibility in his famous analysis of *Mein Kampf,* where he was prompted to ask, "What kind of medicine has this medicine-man concocted?" Burke believed that Hitler's doctrine of the master race was offered as a cure-all for an ailing Germany. The Germans were "a people in collapse, suffering under economic frustration and the defeat of nationalistic aspirations, with the very midrib of their integrative efforts (the army) in a state of dispersion."[35] Burke pointed out that the identity needs of the Germans were parallel to Hitler's own,

25

as he was "suffering under the alienation of poverty and confusion, yearning for some integrative core."[36] The brunt of Burke's analysis is that in Hitler's rhetoric we can see how "Hitler's 'sinister' powers of persuasion derived from the fact that he spontaneously evolved his 'cure-all' in response to inner necessities."[37]

It is of course impossible to summarize Burke's critical evidence for making his claim. But the important thrust is that the text of *Mein Kampf* can be read as a curative rhetoric for Hitler personally *and* for Germans coping with their individual situations. The national or racial identity offered in the rhetoric, and the integration or success that it envisioned, was sufficient to motivate individuals to participate in its enactment. Burke points up the therapeutic rationale by which the rhetoric worked: It is not that Hitler's persuasion implanted a set of ideas in the German people and so changed them from one identity to another. Instead, Burke argues, Hitler's rhetoric provided a "world-view for people who had previously seen the world but piecemeal," and "had no other [world view] to pit against it."[38]

Conventional wisdom and traditional theories of persuasion cling to notions of the "great persuader." People tend to mystify the charismatic qualities of a leader in order to explain mass devotion and to have some way of allocating praise or blame for the effects of persuasion. The Jonestown case evoked such reactions. Several hundred people were allegedly driven to mass suicide by their surrender to the charismatic Rev. Jim Jones. Outsiders typically interpreted such behavior as the effects of Jones' "brainwashing" powers, and many suggested that such coercive persuasion should somehow be made illegal. This response of course oversimplifies what must have happened. Burke's perspective would suggest that one ask *why* persons can see self-destruction as viable action. Many of Jones' followers resembled Hoffer's profile of "true believers"; they too were "poor, misfits, outcasts, minorities, adolescent youth." They felt they had no power to improve their lots in society, and so with Jones they set out to form a new society in which they did have identities of worth and potential for influencing their environment. Up to some point in time, at least, Jones' rhetoric gave them a technique for persuading self, others, and their environment. When it appeared that their new world would be destroyed, their failure was absolute. Only through some absolute redemption could they preserve the spiritual significance they had newly acquired. Perhaps not all Jonestowners went to their deaths without force, but many were *persuaded* to do so.

To conceive that Hitler, Jones, or any other charismatic leader can sweep audiences unheedingly or wholly irrationally into mass action is to

26

ignore the choices that those audiences conceived of themselves as having. When persuasion occurs, what *alternatives* to being persuaded does an individual have? When, as with the Germans and Jonestowners, abject failure and the destruction of one's meaningful identity is emphasized as the only possible alternative, even mass homicide or mass suicide appears to be a viable choice. "Viable," however, only if one recognizes the pragmatic purposes such people have for rhetorically constructing their realities in the first place.

Again we confront one of Burke's important insights: "mortification" (a suicidal impulse) and "victimage" (a homicidal impulse) are but extreme variants of normal ways that people confront failure. Failures are defined with reference to one's view of the world, and symbolic ways of dealing with failure are prescribed within the dramatism of one's world view.[39] The news of the day contains many examples of homicide and suicide as dramatic responses to failure, while film, television, and traditional drama offer countless more. When people come to see their situations as dramatic, it is not impossible to understand why they sometimes enact such symbolic solutions.

Leon Festinger's theory of cognitive dissonance explains less radical choices than those of the Germans or Jonestowners. The basic assumption of Festinger's theory is that people are significantly, perhaps even primarily, motivated to maintain consistency among their "cognitive elements." Those elements come from beliefs and behaviors. When conflict among them occurs, the individual has the choice of changing "the least resistant element." Again in Festinger's theory we find the concept of a self who seeks to integrate beliefs and actions in order to have a consistent and viable identity. In Festinger's view this reintegration is achieved by acts of self-persuasion or persuasion of others.

Details of Festinger's theory have been challenged, but the main thrust of his model has been adopted in the practical study of persuasion. The model essentially points out that persuasive messages can heighten the dissonance between significant elements of one's cognitive makeup and can, in turn, prescribe beliefs or behaviors that serve to reduce dissonance. This theory makes three important contributions for conceiving of persuasion as therapeutic: First, persuading and being persuaded are both motivated by a problem in individual coping; motives for persuasion are self-directed. Second, the desire for integration of self is a response to a situation where disintegration exists or is possible; failure is possible or likely. Third, the strategies and symbols used in persuasion both create and resolve dissonance; failure can be either created or resolved by means of persuasion.

If it seems unfair to call the sources of "inconsistency" failures, recall that Festinger's original dissonance theory grew from a study of a group whose integrating prophecy had failed to come true.[40] Festinger's group had prophesied world disaster. When the prophecy did not come true, the group did not disband; it began to seek out symbolic ways of providing personal and group coherence. Festinger noticed that the members of the group had not expressed commitment to the group nor tried to proselytize for the prophecy of doom and salvation until *after* their prophecy did not come true. According to Festinger, this was because the individuals experienced "dissonance" between the failure of the prophecy and the behavioral commitment they had made by participating in the group and listening to and believing in the prophecy. Also according to Festinger, formation of group coherence and commitment, and subsequent acts of persuasion on behalf of the prophecy, served to reduce the dissonance.

Studies of protest rhetoric have made the self-directed and dissonance-reducing motives for persuasion especially clear. Comparing the protest rhetoric of the Yippies with the "diatribes" of the ancient Cynics, Windt pointed out that persuasion that radically assaults its audience is not ostensibly performed in order to win the audience's favor.[41] But enacting such rhetoric can support the protesters' beliefs, solidify the social support within their groups, and reduce their own anxieties about their apparent powerlessness in the face of evils. These rhetorical exercises give people roles in life, ways of acting, and modes of public expression; they affirm commitments to beliefs that often make these people failures in the eyes of the social majority.

By studying the texts of various protest speeches of the 1960s, Richard B. Gregg similarly identified an "ego-function" of this discourse.[42] Through address and action the protesters' rhetoric affirmed and sustained their identities. Rhetorical action gives reality to and opportunities for enacting one's preferred identity. Aaron D. Gresson expanded on Gregg's analysis to show the importance of intragroup rhetoric in constructing group identities for persons who sense they share class disabilities.[43] And one may point to many recent groups that address issues in terms of class identity: being woman, being black, being gay, being young, being gray, or being Christian. Many groups wishing to change society find that building group identity is a necessary means of acquiring persuasive power in society. But, as for the Germans of the Hitler experience, group identity also serves individuals who seek integration and effective personal identities.

The explosion of "support groups" also attests to the ego-function of rhetoric. Here, as in a movement or protest group, an individual is provided with an analysis of and/or opportunity to analyze the generic problem that the group's members share. A member is given persuasive role models to instruct him or her in interpersonal and public communicative techniques that deal with the problem. The group provides a sympathetic audience that is also instructed in the same styles of communication, for whom and with whom one can be persuasive and thus achieve support. Alcoholics Anonymous, Weight Watchers, diet farms, stress-management seminars, success and personal excellence seminars, all explore the experience of failure and supply techniques for its management. Therapy seminars such as *est* operate along similar lines by having people "protest" the sources and symptoms of their diverse individual ailments. One psychologist has found that he can treat his patients' depression by having them give impromptu speeches. He has found that exercising influence toward the environment through speech gives patients a point at which to begin building senses of personal power and effectiveness, even without a particular cause or belief to espouse.[44]

Support groups for people dealing with particular traumas clearly indicate the therapeutic uses of discourse: One must recover an identity that has been denied by rape, divorce, loss of spouse or family member, and so on. In effect, one must through discourse create a new identity capable of dealing with one's new reality, and one must be able to get support for this new identity through effective communicative techniques. Having the opportunity to *enact* this identity and achieve successful results is a crucial part of the recovery process. The rhetorical experience associated with the stages of the recovery process are clearly therapeutic.

If one's psychosocial identity must manage personal and social pressures through communication, it is perhaps inaccurate ever to speak of one's identity as a fixed or static entity. If self-change is possible, then it must be conceived of as a process wherein (1) one's personal situation, (2) one's received messages, (3) one's own persuasive actions, and (4) the reinforcements that are available combine to produce a new public identity that, if successfully performed and rewarded, becomes a new orientation from which to act. Whether it is a victim of "brainwashing," a novitiate in the *est* program, or a returnee from a religious revival, a person who claims to be displaying a "new" identity is in the act of forming that identity through rhetorical appeal. The success of that appeal, in competition with other factors, will determine the degree of change that is finally accomplished.

The much publicized case of Patty Hearst helps to illustrate how this perspective applies to cases of overt persuasion. Hearst was allegedly abducted, kept in a closet for some 54 days, and then emerged as a member of the radical group that had abducted her. Hearst's first public appearance after being abducted was in a bank robbery. She wore the garb of the group, claimed her name was Tanya and posed with an automatic weapon while the group robbed the bank.

Hearst's actions as Tanya were taken by the public and by the courts as evidence that she had joined the group and was, in every substantive way, a member of the group and therefore responsible for her actions. Hearst claims, however, that she did not "believe" in the group and their cause until *after* the bank robbery, when she "gave up hope of ever getting home, of ever having a normal life again." She recalls thinking that "I was part of the SLA, so I may as well just drill with them, and commit myself in a very real sense, and just give up."[45]

Hearst's account of her state of mind during the ordeal indicates that her actions were therapeutic responses to an intolerable situation, not a passive acceptance of the group's ideology. Hearst says that "if they had come in and said, 'Now we want you to become terribly impassioned over the plight of chocolate doughnuts, because they are so abused,' I would have felt just as impassioned over chocolate doughnuts as I did about the people, because it wouldn't have made any difference to me."

It is an error in cases such as this to assume, as did the jury, that Hearst's performance as Tanya represented a willful change of herself into another person. It also seems an error to believe, as the brainwashing theory of defense psychiatrists implied, that she was a passive victim of powerful messages and techniques of persuasion.[46] Typically, people do not have identities capable of functioning successfully in such extreme circumstances, and both their acceptance of ideological persuasion and their subsequent actions are tentative enactments—part of a process of recovering or reforming an effective identity by dealing with the situations, groups, and personal experiences with which they are confronted. Brainwashers' arguments are usually designed to produce a sense of failure and guilt in the individual. The means of persuasion contained in the verbal message then become means of persuasion that the brainwashee can use to gain approval and survive.

To understand how persuasion operates therapeutically, it is important to appreciate the *active* involvement of individuals undergoing self-change. People do not respond passively to messages. People *use* the contents and strategies of messages to solve problems for themselves. A message can intensify or redefine a particular problem and thus cause people to seek solutions more actively, but persuasive messages usually communicate possibilities for mastering problems. The evidence is especially sharp that where acceptance and validation for one's identity is involved, persuadees appropriate from others' persuasion the means by which *they* legitimize the messages. As J. A. C. Brown points out, what people already believe supplies the chief criteria that determine whether they will take seriously a message directed to them. He writes:

> In group psychotherapy the individual confesses his "sins" and is "pardoned," becomes integrated with a social body, thus accepting the norms it painfully works out for itself, and discovers in interaction with others a revelation of himself. All of these are useful therapeutic results in those who have hitherto felt cut off from society. But they are employed in other fields, too. For example, it has been found in industry that incentive wage plans offering bonuses to individual workers often do more harm than good, whereas group incentives in which the bonus is based upon the work of the whole team are likely to be effective, and even more so when the workers' groups are allowed to discuss plans together and set their own targets of production. The reason for this is that a target which has been set by the members of the group themselves becomes "ego-involved" for each individual.[47]

As Brown's observation indicates, it is not just individual reward that is sought; "reward" entails recognition and involvement.

Social learning theory is strong on this point: success in performing a task or gaining a reward is not sufficient to solidify learning; the person must also believe that the success was directly caused by his or her actions.[48] In other words, people need to be actively involved in producing the results for an experience to be persuasive to them. Even when an individual succeeds in enacting changed identity, there is no lasting change in identity or behaviors if social reinforcement of the behaviors is removed. A new identity must have new and effective rhetorical techniques, and those are supplied in the acts of persuasion in which a person *participates*.

Viewing persuasion as therapeutic leads one to consider that (1) enacting the real or imagined roles or techniques that are urged in a message is fundamental to being persuaded; (2) ego-involving and social rewards tend to fix changed attitudes, behaviors, or identities; and (3) self-change is more than a response to a message, but involves the ways people *use* messages to persuade self, influence environment or the perception of it, or succeed by persuading others.

The above considerations lead to several general conclusions. First, persuasion can contribute to meaningful changes of identity. Second, rhetoric from outside the self cannot alone accomplish such persuasion. Rhetoric from others can, however, evoke or intensify senses of inadequacy and can point to and advocate solutions. Herbert W. Simons sums up what contemporary research suggests about what persuasion from others can accomplish: "The job of persuaders is first to create psychological imbalance in the person they seek to persuade, and then to 'close off' undesired rebalancing mechanisms while simultaneously promoting the resolutions they favor."[49] Third, imbalance is or can be created by definitions and reinforcements of failure, or can be experienced as such. If either is the case, resolutions can be and often are presented as involving a change of personal identity. It is possible that a person's perceived fault or circumstances are so exacerbating and the motivation for "rebalancing" so enthusiastic that the person seeks complete identity change even though messages received do not directly call for identity change.

When rhetoric operates in these fashions, we can reasonably call the rhetoric "therapeutic." This implies that the rhetorical activities of the persuaders and/or persuadees are addressed to healing or repairing some perceived flaw in self. Urging alteration of identity or self-image is a prominent contemporary style of therapy. It appears in three common forms: (1) rhetoric that attempts to put a person or persons in a perceived position of needing therapy; (2) rhetoric that attempts to address and provide remedies for problems assumed already to exist in the audience; (3) rhetoric that both creates the need for and supplies the appropriate therapy.

There are of course many varieties of rhetoric that operate with a therapeutic rationale. These include therapeutic formats that are traditional and forms of rhetoric not often viewed as persuasive in nature. Traditional epideictic speech is largely if not wholly therapeutic in design: eulogies, surrender speeches, apologies, confessions, proclamations, credos, and the like are typically attempts to define, ameliorate, or in some way resolve potential or actual failures. In medicine, myth, religion, drama, and narrative there exist cultural traditions of healing through shared symbols. These are found in incantations, magical preachments, communion, initiations, prayer, and celebration. When these forms of talk are examined as responses to specific and general failings, one is able to consider how they persuade by means of therapeutic processes.

Other forms of therapeutic persuasion are less obviously so. For example, a plethora of television commercials show consumers responding favorably after trying a different bath soap, toothpaste, or home product. Actors typically display their suffering from some embarrassment with family, job, or love life. The actors then display how a successful person talks and feels upon having resolved the problem. The persuasive design of such messages operates with the same basic therapeutic rationale as more extreme cases of failure and response. These messages enact the entire sequence of failure and resolution so that the viewer may participate in a well-worn pattern of persuasion.

Kenneth Burke has explored the various dramatistic modes in which experience of the therapeutic formula can be persuasive. Writing of the "inspirational literature" of 1941 (forerunners to contemporary self-help books), Burke theorized:

> The reading of a book on the attaining of success is in itself the symbolic attaining of that success. It is *while they read* that these readers are "succeeding." . . . The lure of the book resides in the fact that the reader, while reading it, is then living in the aura of success. What he wants is *easy* success; and he gets it in symbolic form by the mere reading itself.[50]

As all of Burke's literary criticism helps to point out, identifying the therapeutic rationale of a work helps to explain how such works operate to gain the identification and participation of the reader. It is in this fashion that Burke sees literature providing us with "equipment for living."

Constructing or exacerbating senses of failure is a common strategy of all persuasive modes. It occurs in normal public speaking, in interpersonal persuasion, in traditional forms of epideictic, in protest speaking, in brainwashing, and in communication with direct or overt therapeutic purposes. Depiction and enactment of failure are chief resources of the dramatist's art; failure is formulaic in literature and autobiography, popular psychology, and advertising. Definition and interpretation of failure are means of religious persuasion, and are central to our modes of socialization and education.

THE DIVIDED SELF

The curative or healing rationales of therapeutic rhetoric attempt to unify the self. Such rhetoric, as we have seen, often helps to promote the idea that the self is flawed and so is in need of unity or repair. We might therefore ask how it is that the self comes to accept the premise that it is flawed and so is led to seek out solutions that promise self-unification.

When we ask where individuals acquire their theories of self, we can answer by pointing to the predominant conceptions of self that are institutionalized in social lore. Psychological theory is an important source and, as Burke helped to point out, the psychologism of literature, drama, and other media also offers models and conceptions of failed and of effective identities. The two leading authoritative sources of therapy in modern society are psychiatry and religion, and they are likewise our two primary sources of theories about self. They diagnose and prescribe identities in and through their therapeutic discourse.

The theme of the divided self is consistent throughout both psychological and religious rhetoric. William James saw the divided self as a "double-storied mystery" in twice-born religious converts. R. D. Laing observes the divided self in cases of schizophrenia, and he argues that this condition is just an extreme failure of normal attempts to maintain an effective and complete sense of selfhood.[51] Paul Ricoeur conceived of failure as a " 'rift' in man, what enables him to 'err,' become divided against himself and thereby to become the 'flawed' creature."[52] The divided self is a patent theme in existential literature and psychoanalytic theorizing. In all these cases we see motivation for symbolic healing deriving from a conception of the self as divided and in need of unification and reintegration.

In Judeo-Christian religion, psychiatry, existential philosophy, and social lore taken generally, we find ontologies of self-division. The basic condition of existence is characterized as one of conflict within self, where self must choose and act in ways that achieve morality, authenticity, genuine being, or success—or in ways that fail to do so. Failure is therefore an integral element of the basic identity that we are given in our cultural theories. People are socialized to recognize the various kinds of failure, and they are socialized to respond to failure with motivation for repair. Guilt is normally what we call the experience of feeling personally responsible for conditions that we recognize as failure. Guilt is also, however, a sense that we must respond to those conditions to make repairs.

Kenneth Burke understood the rhetorical significance of our ontologies of failure and guilt. For instance, he saw "original sin" as a basic interpretation that causes us to take to ourselves responsibility for acting toward division or separation in the world. Through original sin, Burke thought, the individual internalizes the basic separation between self and other, or self and God, and is thus motivated to seek solutions that create identification through rhetoric. In all of these therapeutic and symbolic analyses of motivation we find this basic pattern: Human identity is defined as divided and capable of failure; the self internalizes "fault" for flawed conditions and thus experiences them as proof of its division and failure; to repair this flawed identity the individual must seek out symbolic resolutions—those provided by therapeutic rhetorics found in religion, psychiatry, psychology, or, as I have sought to point out, the general rhetorical involvements available in social persuasion.

Burke also grasped another important fact useful to an analysis of failure and guilt. The basic theories of identity prescribed by our therapeutic institutions are tautological. We are given a divided self, one defined as capable of failure or success, and are socialized to respond with motivation for repair. It can be, then, that feeling responsible or feeling that there are means for repair causes one to search for how one has failed. Rhetoricians have made this basic reflex into an art of persuasion. To the extent that one can show means of resolving a problem, one can get the audience to feel responsible and ultimately feel like failures if they do not respond. This, again, is a basic hypothesis of cognitive dissonance theory.

Aristotle seems to have recognized the rhetorical usefulness of this pattern in his analysis of "shame" as a rhetorical *topos*. Shame is of course not identical to post-Christian and post-Freudian guilt, but its rhetorical functions are the same. Aristotle defined shame as "a pain or disturbance in regard to bad things, whether present, past, or future, which seem likely to involve us in discredit."[53] We feel shame in reference to those people with whom we identify and whom we would expect to feel shame in reference to ourselves. Aristotle conceived of shame as "a mental picture of disgrace, in which we shrink from the disgrace itself and not its consequences."[54] In other words, we experience psychological pain in response to a socialized image of disgrace; that pain motivates us to attempt to restore our standing in both our own eyes and the eyes of others.

Rhetorical treatment of shame can evoke the "mental picture of disgrace" and thus motivate the remedial responses desired. Aristotle's shame involves concern for the opinions of others and concern for one's perceived status. This mental picture is much different from guilt, which more clearly reveals the divided self. Guilt implies that one is guilty toward the higher or better part of oneself and, as Ricoeur says, that one is "ready to undergo the chastisement and to make oneself the subject of the chastisement."[55] Although the mental picture and the socially recognized circumstances which prescribe shame or guilt are different, the motivational conditioning is the same: One is given, as part of identity, the responsibility for responding to shameful or guilty conditions with remedial actions.

The rhetorical structure of guilt is implied in contemporary psychiatrist Robert J. Lifton's analysis. Lifton sees guilt as "the broken connection," or the disruption of important relationships between people and the world, and he believes that this concept should be the new paradigm of motivation. He defines guilt in general as "an image-feeling of responsibility or blame for bringing about injury or disintegration, or other psychological equivalents of death."[56] This interpretation of guilt has little to do with the judgments of others or the standards of social evaluation. It emphasizes the important connections sought among personal identity, the world, and desire for self-importance and influence. As in Aristotle's idea of shame, an "image" of guilt is associated with a "feeling" of pain or disturbance, but the grounds of the experience are the integration of individual identity with the world and the individual's ability to manage the events of the world. Lifton writes that "guilt is experienced as expression of, and responsibility for, the breakdown of social balance, and an indication of threat to individual centering and grounding."[57] Shame implies responsiveness to others; guilt, in this psychological view, implies a responsiveness to personal needs for an effective identity.

Whether the primary guides to one's identity come from religion, psychology, or social convention, the tautological relationship of failure and guilt is the same. Guilt is already defined *in theory* as a universal human motivation. Each instance of maladjustment or personal inadequacy therefore becomes an instance which we interpret as guilt and proceed to repair as guilt. Prominent psychological and religious doctrines have worked out this tautological way of defining and treating conditions of failure, and their formulations have supplied acculturated ways of conceptualizing psychic remediation. The result is a set of shared conceptions and languages for dealing with failures of all sorts.

This symbolic relationship among failure, identity, and guilt indicates a fundamental operation of therapeutic rhetoric. Whatever one's specific failure happens to be, or whatever particular feelings of responsibility one has, therapeutic rhetoric allows one to reduce these matters to one essential cause and one basic response. Therapeutic theories promote a fundamental definition and interpretation of what basic flaw divides the self. When we encounter situations of failure, we can and often do employ these theories to interpret our situations. In theory, the pain or disturbance we feel is given one basic character—guilt.

The experience of guilt implies, in Lifton's terms, that our connections with the world have been ruptured and are in need of repair. We then seek out remedial solutions that must not only repair problems in the world, but must also repair our own divided or flawed identities. The solutions must, in some symbolic fashion, provide this therapy. It is therefore therapeutic to be persuaded that problems indeed come from one basic flaw in one's personal identity. Persons are willing to generalize and symbolize their particular failing according to the prescriptions of such theory because the theory recommends a rhetorical solution to the problem of identity. This basic tautology is implicit within the rationale of therapeutic rhetoric.

The world is seen by all of us as a place where failure is at least possible. Treatment of self and world may, as in Christian theology, specify that failure is inevitable or necessary to spiritual being. Or, failure may be viewed as human fate or as the consequence of a random world where humans are, in theory, without fault. Even in the latter case, effective ways of dealing with failure require that persons respond to the conditions that damage them. Therapeutic rhetoric will be created, and this rhetoric will presuppose that repair can come about through reformation of self by alignment with and obedience to some theory of self, world, and their proper relationship.

Finally, I wish to emphasize that failure, identity, and guilt are all matters that can be negotiated and redefined. Whether a social or personal situation does or does not constitute failure, what the character of the failure is, what and who are responsible and why, what kind and degree of responsibility is had or shared, and what the appropriate responses are, are all questions about which talk is made and answers are produced in rhetorical discourse.

NOTES

1. Kenneth Burke, *Towards a Better Life* (1932; rpt. Berkeley: University of California Press, 1966), 40.
2. Eric Hoffer, *The True Believer* (New York: Harper, 1951), 24.

3. Marilyn Ferguson, *The Aquarian Conspiracy: Personal and Social Transformation in the 1980s* (Los Angeles: J. P. Tarcher, 1980); Thomas J. Peters and Robert H. Waterman, Jr., *In Search of Excellence: Lessons from America's Best Run Companies* (New York: Harper, 1982).

4. Ferguson, 25.

5. Ferguson, 25; her emphasis.

6. Peters and Waterman, xxi.

7. Ferguson, 35.

8. Peters and Waterman, 10.

9. Jimmy Carter, *A Government as Good as Its People* (New York: Simon and Schuster, 1977), 243.

10. Ferguson, 36.

11. Tom Wolfe, "The 'Me' Decade and the Third Great Awakening," *New York*, Aug. 23, 1976: 26–40.

12. Richard Sennett, *The Fall of Public Man* (New York: Random House, 1978); Christopher Lasch, *The Culture of Narcissism* (New York: Norton, 1979).

13. See Walter J. Ong, *Hopkins, the Self, and God* (Toronto: University of Toronto Press, 1986).

14. Robert M. Bellah, et al., *Habits of the Heart: Individualism and Commitment in American Life* (Berkeley: University of California Press, 1985), 83–84.

15. William Barrett, *The Illusion of Technique* (Garden City, NY: Doubleday, 1978).

16. Roy F. Baumeister, *Identity: Cultural Change and the Struggle for Self* (New York: Oxford University Press, 1986), 246.

17. Baumeister, 247.

18. Baumeister, 4.

19. Baumeister, 4.

20. Erving Goffman, *Asylums: Essays on the Social Situation of Mental Patients and Other Inmates* (Chicago: Aldine, 1962); *Presentation of Self in Everyday Life* (Garden City, NY: Doubleday, 1959); *Relations in Public* (New York: Harper, 1972); *Stigma: Notes on the Management of Spoiled Identity* (Englewood Cliffs, NJ: Prentice Hall, 1963).

21. Erving Goffman, "On Cooling the Mark Out: Some Aspects of Adaptation to Failure," *Psychiatry* 15 (1952): 462.

22. Goffman, "On Cooling," 462.

23. Goffman, "On Cooling," 462.

24. Erik Erikson, *Dimensions of a New Identity* (New York: Norton, 1974); *Identity and the Life Cycle* (Norton, 1980); *Life History and the Historical Moment* (Norton, 1975).

25. Erikson, *Life History*, 20.

26. Peter L. Berger and Thomas Luckmann, *The Social Construction of Reality: A Treatise in the Sociology of Knowledge* (Garden City, NY: Doubleday, 1967).

27. Berger and Luckmann, 60–62, 129–30.

28. Ch. Perelman and L. Olbrechts-Tyteca, *The New Rhetoric: A Treatise on Argumentation* (Notre Dame, IN: University of Notre Dame Press, 1969), 51.

29. Alasdair MacIntyre, *A Short History of Ethics* (New York: Macmillan, 1966), 7.

30. MacIntyre, 8.

31. Goffman, "On Cooling," 453.

32. Goffman, "On Cooling," 461.

33. Kenneth Burke, *Attitudes Toward History* (1937; rpt. Berkeley: University of California Press, 1985).

34. Kenneth Burke, *A Rhetoric of Motives* (1950; rpt. Berkeley: University of California Press, 1969), esp. 19–27, 55–59.

35. Kenneth Burke, *Philosophy of Literary Form* (1941; rpt. Berkeley: University of California Press, 1973), 205.

36. Burke, *Philosophy,* 200.

37. Burke, *Philosophy,* 211.

38. Burke, *Philosophy,* 218.

39. See Kenneth Burke, *The Rhetoric of Religion* (1961; rpt. Berkeley: University of California Press, 1970), 190–191. The analysis of "mortification" and "victimage" runs throughout his work.

40. Leon Festinger, et al., *When Prophecy Fails* (1956; rpt. New York: Harper, 1964).

41. Theodore Otto Windt, "The Diatribe: Last Resort for Protest," *Quarterly Journal of Speech* 58 (1972): 1–14.

42. Richard B. Gregg, "The Ego-Function of the Rhetoric of Protest," *Philosophy & Rhetoric* 4 (1972): 71–91.

43. Aaron D. Gresson, "Minority Epistemology and the Rhetoric of Creation," *Philosophy & Rhetoric* 10 (1977): 244–62.

44. Martin E. P. Seligman, "Fall into Helplessness," *Psychology Today,* June 1973: 43–48. See also his book, *Helplessness: On Depression, Development, and Death* (San Francisco: Freeman, 1975).

45. Patty Hearst, in a television interview with Barbara Walters, ABC *20/20,* Dec. 10, 1981 (transcript, p. 4). For reference, see Patty Hearst, with Alvin Moscow, *Every Secret Thing* (Garden City, NY: Doubleday, 1982); Kenneth J. Reeves, *The Trial of Patty Hearst* (San Francisco: Great Fidelity Press, 1976); and Philip G. Zimbardo, et al., *Influencing Attitudes and Changing Behavior* (Reading, MA: Addison-Wesley, 1977), 4–15.

46. See Thomas Szasz, "Patricia Hearst's Psychiatrists: Twice Brainwashed," *The New Republic,* Oct. 23, 1976: 6–8.

47. J. A. C. Brown, *Techniques of Persuasion* (Baltimore: Penguin Books, 1963), 206–7.

48. See Julian B. Rotter, "External and Internal Control," *Psychology Today,* June 1971: 37. See also Rotter, et al., *Applications of a Social Learning Theory of Personality* (New York: Holt, Rinehart, 1972).

49. Herbert W. Simons, *Persuasion: Understanding, Practice, and Analysis* (Reading, MA: Addison-Wesley, 1976), 17.

50. Burke, "Literature as Equipment for Living," in *Philosophy,* 299.

51. R. D. Laing, *The Divided Self* (New York: Random House, 1969).

52. Charles Kelbley, foreword to Ricoeur's *Fallible Man,* trans. Charles Kelbley (Chicago: Regnery, 1965), xiii.

53. Aristotle, *Rhetoric,* trans. W. Rhys Roberts (New York: Random House, 1954), 14–18.

54. Aristotle, 23–24.
55. Paul Ricoeur, *The Symbolism of Evil,* trans. Emerson Buchanan (New York: Harper, 1967), 101–2.
56. Robert J. Lifton, *The Broken Connection* (New York: Simon and Schuster, 1980), 139.
57. Lifton, 144–45.

3

MANAGING FAILURE THROUGH TALK

The concept of individual identity as psychosocial implies that individual identity is a symbolic phenomenon. This, in turn, implies that identity is of a species with other symbols and that its psychosocial dimensions are products of symbolic interaction. Identity is visibly negotiated and mediated in communicative activities where the dialectical relation of personality and social experience is established and sustained.

I have argued that interactions undertaken to avoid and reconcile failure are episodes where the rhetorical and symbolic nature of identity are displayed and addressed. I have noted further that in treatments of human failure, a number of scholars conceive of failure as an experience wherein a person's identity or sense of self is divided. That is, the symbolization of identity during times of failure reveals a divided, fragmented, or inconsistent construction, such that an individual's communicative activities are focused on achieving some sense or character of self as individual. Both scholarship and common sense support the view that the unity and harmony of anyone's sense of self are fragile and that events or symbolic conflicts can evoke disharmony and division in one's self-image. Another way of putting this is to say that the experience of self as atomic and indivisible is achieved only at times when one's tensions and divisions are, for the moment, resolved, and that this sense of self exists as a symbolic or mythified goal to be pursued, especially at times of extreme disunity or division.

Discourse that seeks to repair perceived damage to one's self-conception will have the basic structure of identifying the loci of problems and of offering solutions that address those loci—with the goal of restoring a sense of unity and harmony. In such discourse, then, one may expect to find problems conceived in terms of divisions in self and situation, and remedies that provide avenues of unification in self and situation. In this chapter I want to deal with two essential patterns of remediation that occur in discourse that seeks to ameliorate sensed inadequacy or failure.

THE DIALECTIC OF CONSOLATION AND COMPENSATION

When communication is aimed at performing some sort of remedy or therapy for failure, the primary purpose of that communication is rhetorical and can have one or both of two basic functions: to console and/or to open the way for compensation. Let me first explain what is meant by consolation.

Rhetoric can console someone for a loss or hardship for which there is no real remedy. Consolation occurs when some sort of comfort is accepted, usually in the form of a substitute for what has been lost. Some version of consolation is performed when one points to the bright side of things, makes other options seem more desirable than previously they were held to be, offers heaven as a world where present miseries will no longer exist, brings a puppy into the house when the family pet, or even a family member, has passed away, or in any way seeks to lessen rather than vanquish loss. To console is to persuade to a different order of valuations wherein a new perspective on the loss is possible. In consolation, loss is neither denied nor erased. Consolation minimizes and diverts attention from loss and painful consequences.

By contrast, when one compensates, one tries to balance things, to "get even," to find another way to achieve the original goals or something like them, or perhaps to set and gain even better goals. Compensation also can involve substitution, but the substitute is assumed to be equal to or greater than the thing originally sought.

A mundane example can illustrate the difference between consolation and compensation. Some years ago I was surprised to hear a former Mr. America speak on television with a heavy lisp. His amazing physique had landed him a television role—one that had not required him to speak. Now, as a celebrity interviewee, his speech defect could seem to be a kind of failure; it was a flaw in someone whose success was physical perfection. Consider how audiences might think about the incongruity. In this circumstance television viewers could imagine that Mr. America built his physique as a *compensation* for his speech defect. Whatever scholastic, social, or romantic failures he must have suffered could be weighed against his physical and related social accomplishments. After such success Mr. America could trust that his audience would perceive his speech fault as minimal. In situations where success requires normal speech, however, Mr. America's "failure" would still not be erased nor ignored. Despite successful compensation for the flaw by both himself and his audience, it still could lead to undeniable failure that must be consoled. In this latter case, what formerly compensated for failure could become a consolation for him—even though the objective facts about self and society remained the same across situations. The same basic failure can call forth both compensation and consolation, and require different interpretations of the same data.

One can compensate for failure either by taking different routes to a given goal or by repairing the failure and, as it were, starting over again toward one's original goal. One can also compensate for failure by shifting one's criteria for success; e.g., speech patterns do not really count because celebrity can be achieved through other means. However, when one's goal is unobtainable, loss must be accepted and dealt with through consolation. We can, and often we do, console ourselves by choosing different and more readily attainable goals. A failed starting pitcher, for example, may find consolation in victories won in relief. In such cases a different hierarchy of values is embraced though the original loss remains.

The distinction between consolation and compensation is clear, but it seems impossible to find any pure examples of either process. Accepting a consolation prize does involve a balancing; it also involves a definable loss and requires a person to compensate for failure in one endeavor by accepting success in another endeavor. Compensation also involves recognizing at some point that a failure is undeniable. Other means and ends are substituted as sufficient to console for the loss and then compensate for the failure with equal or greater success. Consolation and compensation are concomitant functions in most episodes of managing failure. They are dialectically related as the logic of failure dictates. Rhetorically they are two different postures toward an interpretation of failure. The two postures may, of course, be taken at different times and in different situations, addressing the same failure. For example, to one's friends one may compensate for losing a job by talking about greater opportunities, or by claiming that the boss or company is at fault, or by asserting that one actually quit or is glad to have lost the job. However true such claims are, the lost job will be an undeniable failure, perhaps in the eyes of one's spouse or family or in one's own mind. If so, consolation will be needed, and that consolation for oneself may be composed of the same claims offered to one's friends as compensatory. The differences are in one's position in the situation, the definition and value given to what has been lost by self or social group, and the persuasive purpose of the dialectical move one makes. With one's friends one compensates to maintain or rebuild one's self-image, for that is what is risked. With one's family and oneself status is perhaps not risked, but the loss of a meaningful role, income, or other values of the job is undeniable and therefore some consolation must be performed.

Consolation and compensation occur when anyone deals with failure. We often console others, and as the Mr. America example suggests, an audience or friend often must help with or agree to the terms of effective compensation. In the instance of an employer dismissing an employee, it will often occur that the dismissal is delivered in ways that frame possible avenues of consolation or compensation or even directly suggest them. The employer can minimize the degree of the employee's fault, or exonerate the employee of all blame. Consolation can be offered by pointing out strengths of the individual or future opportunities, or by stating that the reasons for the dismissal have hurt other good employees as well. The two points to be noted are that whoever deals with potential or actual failure must also deal with the associated losses, and in dealing with those losses any participant will aim at some combination of consolation and compensation. The two kinds of responses are persuasive in purpose and undeniably rhetorical.

Traditional rhetorical theory conceives that systematic address to familiar issues and arguments evolves standard themes, and that these themes represent the basic cultural knowledge about and pragmatic means of dealing with such issues. The Greeks called these *topoi* (singular, *topos*), meaning the "place" one goes to discover the available ideas and arguments that are likely to be persuasive on the given topic. The idea that such *topoi* have evolved from the rhetorical history of each subject or persuasive purpose makes *topos* far more useful here than the English word "topic." The *topoi* for managing failure reveal the traditional ways of performing consolation and compensation. I suggest that they also show us how failure is culturally and symbolically observed, and how failure is defined in such ways that cooperative resolutions via discourse are possible.

My central contention through the remainder of this book is that *perceived or sensed failure creates rhetorical situations that require the purposes of consolation and compensation, and that these purposes are executed by drawing lines of argument, assertion, and response from a set of basic* topoi *that constantly recur in therapeutic rhetoric.* In this and later chapters I hope to show that three dialectical pairs of *topoi* identify the basic patterns of both contemporary and historical discourse about failure. The pairs of *topoi* are self–society, past–future, and spiritual–material. There may be more specific and varied ways that a

44

topical analysis of responses to failure could be performed, but these basic *topoi* elucidate the symbolic and dialectical ways of conceiving and resolving failure. They also demonstrate the essential logic of consolation and compensation.

In its purest form, consolation involves making discourse that emphasizes social value over personal loss, conditions and causes of the past over present failing, and spiritual meanings or orientations over material losses. In its purest form, compensatory discourse stresses self-directed involvements or motives, future consequences or opportunities, and material values and orientations. One can see the workings of the *topoi* in the basic example I have been using. When a discharged employee, the boss, or the family of the employee are involved in consoling, they will stress themes that minimize the individual's fault and stress possible benefits. They may argue that the failure has social causes and that the conditions of the loss are rooted in the past; the causes are therefore undeniable and unchangeable and must be accepted. Such consolers may argue that the failure represents a spiritual success or value that is more enduring or desirable than the material aspects of the lost job. Having consoled in such ways, any of the parties may seek to identify compensations for the loss. To do so they will point to the self-interests of the failed person, perhaps by showing that he or she now has new opportunities. Or it may be argued that there is some material gain despite the spiritual discouragement connected with the loss—for example, saying there are ways the employee can now earn more money and do so without having to tolerate the old situation. In each such case compensation is performed by redefining the situation in a way that tends to erase the loss and transform it into an opportunity for gain.

My claim is that it is entirely logical that consolation and compensation should be the primary modes of response to failure. Consolation involves dissociating the individual from the loss, emphasizing other persons, past successes, and spiritual gains or substitutes for the material loss. (In the last connection, it is common in our culture to believe that failure can engender spiritual growth.) Compensation emphasizes individual involvement, future possibilities for change or repair, and material gain. There is a sense in which consolation is a spiritual enterprise and compensation a material one. Consolation is performed by and with others; compensation focuses on personal quest. Consolation looks back at the loss and proposes adaptations to that past. Compensation looks forward to future ways of balancing or eliminating or overcoming the loss.

This, I contend, is the logic of response to failure. I propose to show that the *topoi* I have identified and their use in consolation and compensation inhere in all responses to failure.

The use of failure and its consequences as criteria for evaluating identity is as old as the use of praise and blame in rhetorical modes of socialization. One is reminded of Demosthenes' closing in *On the Crown*, where he answers Aeschines' charges by saying, "To err in nothing and to succeed in all things is the prerogative of gods. Why then, accursed man, do you rail at me for my failures?"

Yet the last twenty years of political and rhetorical experience in America have specially educated the public to the ways that failure can be expressed and managed in public speech. Contemporary Americans have seen leaders and ideals falter and sometimes fall, and those events have had to be managed through public rhetoric. Social criticism has not failed to notice the ritualistic elements of how contemporary leaders and their discourse treat failure. The popular music group The Police identify what they term "a rhetoric of failure" in which leaders "subjugate the meanings" of their messages. In this musical mode of social criticism, the group offers the refrain that "we are spirits in a material world" a positive and affirming therapy that uses one of the major *topoi* of consolation and compensation.

The rhetorical efforts to cope with the assassinations of leaders in the past three decades are further instances of rhetorically coping with failures. Some have claimed that a genre of apologetic discourse has emerged in mass-mediated attempts of leaders to repair their public images. President Truman's public defense of his discretion in making appointments, Richard Nixon's famous "Checkers" speech where he defended uses of his campaign fund, Ted Kennedy's responses to Chappaquiddick concerns, and, of course, President Nixon's resignation speech are only the more dramatic instances of the contemporary need to give public accounting of perceived or alleged failures.

The example of the Nixon resignation speech is utterly clear in its uses of compensation and consolation. He said that his public life had been part of "the turbulent history of this era," a consolatory use of the past. His long speech primarily offered compensations for loss for himself and his supporters, emphasizing his personal motives and sacrifices, pointing to the future successes his presidency would be able to claim, and stressing the material value of his presidency despite his own and the nation's spiritual defeat of having a discredited administration.

However much compensation was needed to bolster Nixon's supporters or convince his enemies, the loss was undeniable, especially for

Nixon personally. Predictably, he ended his speech, and his presidential identity, with consolation:

> Sometimes I have succeeded and sometimes I have failed, but always I have taken heart in what Theodore Roosevelt once said about the man in the arena: "whose face is marred by dust and sweat and blood, who strives valiantly, who errs and comes short again and again because there is not effort without error and shortcoming, but who does actually strive to do the deeds, who knows the great enthusiasms, the great devotions, who spends himself in a worthy cause, who at the best knows in the end the triumph of high achievements and who at the worst, if he fails, at least fails while daring greatly."

Nixon's final consolation addresses himself and his image in history. His public identity seemed to be Nixon's lifelong preoccupation, but ironically he suffered repeated public failure. The discourse in this consolatory passage shifts emphasis from a personal to a social perspective, from the future to past precedents of failure, and from material defeats to spiritual goals that were sought and to some degree proven by the failure. As in Demosthenes' epitaph, the inevitability and ubiquity of failure as proven in past pursuits of spiritual achievement is a consolation that diminishes personal failure. This is a frequent pattern of consolatory rhetoric.

No single speech has as deeply influenced our standards of public address in the last two decades as Martin Luther King, Jr.'s "I have a Dream." The speech received a great deal of attention during its twentieth anniversary, and this attention was itself a testimonial to the importance and status of the speech as a cultural symbol. The "dream" has become a shorthand rhetorical expression for civil rights and social ideals generally. This status as a historical and cultural artifact and its repeated symbolic use in political and reformist rhetoric make King's speech especially inviting for analysis.

It may at first seem odd to consider such a successful and inspirational speech an example of rhetoric that deals with failure, or to conceive of King as having to manage failure on the very afternoon when his name was written into our national history. The speech is remembered for its idealism and for its clear statement of the nature of spiritual success in American society, not as a management of failure. But King's idealism and image of spiritual success were responses to a number of recognized and felt failures.

The civil rights movement was troubled with respect to its identity and its leadership. Had the nonviolent approach of King's leadership failed to achieve its goals, and should the movement become more militant as younger leaders urged? Talk of violence had caused mainstream society to question the legitimacy of the movement, and the violence that the blacks themselves had suffered put into question the legitimacy of nonviolent protest. Legislation establishing equal rights for blacks had not been passed, despite the efforts of the movement. A major issue on August 28, 1963, the centennial anniversary of the Emancipation Proclamation, was whether the movement had failed. Where were the much talked-about freedom and equality for blacks in American society? All friends of King's movement knew and felt these failures, and the issue of failure was an important part of the context in which a quarter million people undertook the march on Washington. At the Lincoln Memorial that afternoon, King *had* to deal with actual and potential failures of the movement and their causes, else he would fail as a leader and fail to produce any constructive results through the march.

At a critical juncture in the speech King recognized the audience's feelings of frustration and failure, and he offered consolation:

> I am not unmindful that some of you have come here out of great trials and tribulations. Some of you have come from areas where your quest for freedom left you battered by the storms of persecution and staggered by the winds of police brutality. You have been the veterans of creative suffering. Continue to work with the faith that unearned suffering is redemptive.

King's consolation here is drawn from religious rhetoric, and that style resounds through much of the speech, but this is a crucial point in the speech for other reasons. At this point there was shift from a consolatory to a compensatory posture. The listener was here shifted from a passive sufferer to one who continues to work against suffering. Past suffering can only be redeemed by future struggle. There was a transition from a focus on an alienated and failed collective to a focus on individuals who were being redeemed. From recalling past racial injustice attention was directed to a view from "the mountain" and a call for future actions that could compensate for the past. Material suffering was infused with spiritual meaning and value in both the present and future. Each alternation brought about a shift from the *topoi* of consolation to those of compensation, and examining this shift reveals something about King's purposes and about therapeutic strategies in general.

The relationship of black identity (for King it was still the "Negro") to mainstream American society was the subject of the speech's introduction. Standing before Lincoln's statue, King began by echoing Lincoln's language in "Fivescore years ago," and recalling Lincoln "in whose symbolic shadow we now stand." King recalled the Emancipation Proclamation, the hundred-year-old document that promised a new relationship of blacks to whites. But King observed that "one hundred years later the life of the Negro is still sadly crippled by the manacles of segregation and the chains of discrimination," and "the Negro lives on a lonely island of poverty in the midst of a vast ocean of material prosperity . . . still languishing in the corners of American society and finds himself an exile in his own land." In this definition of the failure that led to this protest, King has used the *topoi* I have identified to show that the problem of discrimination was between the selves of blacks and the character of society; a schism existed between past promise and future freedom; there was a deep contradiction between society's announced spiritual ideals and material reality. King added imagery that would dramatize these dualities and conflicts: the blacks were "exiles" still, living on an "island of poverty" in an "ocean of material prosperity."

The uses of the *topoi* to generate claims, characterizations, and a perspective combined and overlapped. The self–society division that produced a failure for blacks trying to cope with life became a failure for society, as America was measured against its ideals and found at fault. King's message of brotherhood, his desire for integration of blacks and whites, were premised on past and present situations of alienation and segregation. But the conditions of failure became cause for hope: "Now is the time to rise from the dark and desolate valley of segregation to the sunlit path of racial justice." Since the failure belonged to all of society, so did the benefits of its repair: "Now is the time to lift our nation from the quicksands of racial injustice to the solid rock of brotherhood." The statements identified the failure as division, its resolution as unification and brotherhood. Where the failure was cast as a division between self and society, the solution was collective integration; where the failure was cast as schism between past and future, the solution was present change. King's "Now is the time" subtly promised both consolation and compensation. To the whites the phrase urged quick action and compensatory repair; to the blacks the phrase suggested that fulfillment and an end to the suffering was or could be near, consoling them for the loss and urging patience.

The next passage of the speech continued the consolatory address to blacks. It also promised remedy for white fears: "But there is something I must say to my people. . . . We must not allow our creative protest to degenerate into physical violence. Again and again we must rise to the majestic heights of meeting physical force with soul force." King was addressing one of the rifts in the civil rights movement. The strategy was to elevate spiritual values above material losses, consoling blacks for loss and forestalling their desire for compensation through violence. At the same time, the white audience was appealed to, but for them the passage urged a focus on their own material actions and compensation by ending their violence against blacks.

By the end of the speech King had spelled out what has become a legendary vision of brotherhood. That vision was clearly offered as a resolution to the division between black identity and American society. King envisioned that the "sons of former slaves and the sons of former slave-owners will be able to sit together at the table of brotherhood," and that even the state of Alabama will be transformed into a situation where "little black boys and black girls will be able to join hands with little white boys and white girls and walk together as sisters and brothers." In his dream King heard a "beautiful symphony of brotherhood," where we "are able to work together, to pray together, to struggle together," meaning "all of God's children, black men and white men, Jews and Gentiles, Protestants and Catholics, will be able to join hands and sing . . . 'Free at last! Free at last! thank God Almighty, we are free at last!' "

One of the powers of the speech derives from viewing images of segregation, alienation, and self–social conflict through compensatory and consolatory analyses of the conflict, analyses that point toward a final resolution and unification that transforms individuals into a spiritual collective.

Use of the past–future *topos* in the speech reveals the same pattern. The speech began with a symbolic starting point in the history of civil rights, the signing of the Emancipation Proclamation, and by recalling the times of slavery. The early part of the speech recalled the "appalling condition" which the protesters "have come here today to dramatize." Recounting the horror of slavery and the history of the civil rights struggles was consolatory for the black audience, affirming their suffering and the historical roots of their present mission. For the white audience King recalled the commitment of American policy and ideals to racial equality, invoking guilt and opening the way for compensatory argument. He moved from the past to the present, citing the continued conditions of inequality and injustice; then came to the passage I have already examined, where he stressed "the fierce urgency of *now*," repeating the word with emphasis in consecutive lines and insisting that "*now* is the time to make real the promises of democracy." King provided support and faith

50

for his followers while at the same time motivating the white audience toward action. With one of his crystalline metaphors King moved from past to present to future: "It would be fatal for the nation to overlook the urgency of the moment. . . . This sweltering summer of the Negro's legitimate discontent will not pass until there is an invigorating autumn of freedom and equality. 1963 is not an end, but a beginning."

King's use of temporal progression is interesting for several reasons. First, as was common in King's religious style, progression was expressed through naturalistic images and allusions to the passing of the seasons. The references to the past set the stage for both consolatory and compensatory messages, and then the progression was taken as a warrant for turning to the future. The perspective that the sufferers had on the present was transformed in this shift from a present perceived as the "end" of a failed period to the "beginning" of a new future. Up to this point the rationale of the speech was consolatory, recollecting the past in light of present failure. After this point the rationale became compensatory, with King urging his audience to "march ahead" and to "go back" to their states and to continue to work for the envisioned future.

By the time King delivered the peroration beginning with "I have a dream," his listeners had been lifted from the valley of despair to the top of the mountain. In the dream, they were positioned as looking forward to an idealized future. The past history as interpreted had provided a consolatory position for blacks and the basis for compensation by whites. The future King offered provided an ultimate compensation for blacks and a kind of consolation for whites. It did not erase the past, but it gave whites a spiritual success to substitute for their past failures to grant equality.

King steadily drew claims from the spiritual–material *topos*. These are perhaps the most telling indicators of his consolatory and compensatory purposes. Throughout the speech King used spiritual referents for material problems and material referents for spiritual problems. He masterfully set up and maintained tensions between material conditions and spiritual ideals, and offered rhetorical resolutions to those tensions by aligning images of spirit with those of matter. His strategies for accomplishing this bear close attention. King began by advancing spiritual concepts and symbols, citing Lincoln, the Emancipation Proclamation, and the "unalienable rights of life, liberty, and the pursuit of happiness." But he quickly materialized the ideals in a dramatic way. These spiritual ideals demanded prompt "cash" payment:

In a sense we have come to our nation's Capital to cash a check.

When the architects of our republic wrote the magnificent words of the Constitution and the Declaration of Independence, they were signing a promissory note to which every American was to fall heir. . . . It is obvious today that America has defaulted on this promissory note insofar as her citizens of color are concerned. Instead of honoring this sacred obligation, America has given the Negro people a bad check; a check which has come back marked "insufficient funds." But we refuse to believe that the bank of justice is bankrupt. We refuse to believe that there are insufficient funds in the great vaults of opportunity of this nation. So we have come to cash this check—a check that will give us upon demand the riches of freedom and the security of justice.

King's achievement here, as in many other speeches, is memorable, but it is rhetorically striking that he made such a pedestrian metaphor as "bad check" fit in a speech that became noted for its spiritual and stylistic grace. The situation was fraught with spiritual–material paradoxes, and King found a way to integrate the two kinds of qualities. The conditions he was dealing with as evidences of failure were without doubt predominately material conditions, but in his analysis they derived from disregard of ideals. Some urged reaction to the conditions with material violence—a tactic quite different from King's desire to oppose unequal material conditions with a spiritual rededication to idealistic principles. King resolved the antinomy between spiritual and material considerations by forming an equation summed up in the words: "the riches of freedom and the security of justice." Riches and security were portrayed as the products of the ideals of freedom and justice. As he later said, his dream was "deeply embedded in the American dream," as was his equation. Material and spiritual attainments were thus rhetorically bonded, with the result that both blacks and whites presumably could find consolation for their spiritual failures and material compensation for past faults in rewards to be created "now."

King's interconnection between material conditions and spiritual ideals is a common topical pattern in religious rhetoric. But King's rhetoric illustrates other connections between spiritual and material that are interesting. Economic materialism and political idealism, for instance, are not overtly religious. Although his rhetoric was steadily and traditionally spiritual, King always understood that solutions to his people's troubles lay in material and economic equality. He was shot, one recalls, while leading a sanitation workers' strike. In King's use of spiritual–material themes, he could both console and compensate by shifting emphasis from one to the other.

My extended analysis of the King speech is intended to show representative ways in which the *topoi* self–society, past–future, and spiritual–material are drawn upon to generate claims that deal with perceived failures. The analysis also shows how uses of arguments drawn from the *topoi* function to console and/or offer compensations. There are several less obvious conclusions to which my topical analysis points. (1) It is possible for a given rhetorical treatment of failure to offer consolation and/or compensation to more than one audience. King's speech is a clear instance of using the self–society *topos* as a thematic explanation of division and as an articulation of future unification. (2) Because the *topoi* identify dialectically related themes, using arguments and claims drawn from them enables a rhetor to (a) define a failure or failures strategically, and (b) position the rhetor and situated audience in relation to the failure(s). For example, King positions his black audience as injured selves deserving consolation, but he also positions them as capable of achieving compensation. (3) The functions of compensation and consolation tend to become entwined in actual discourse. What yields consolation can also be shown to reveal the avenues to compensation, and vice versa. King interpreted injuries that arose from disregard of ideals as both consolable spiritual failures and compensable material failures. (4) The themes of self–society, past–future, and spiritual–material constitute grounds for defining, redefining, and transforming failures, and for isolating where fault lies and how it is to be interpreted. (5) When definitions and locations of fault have been achieved, the three sets of *topoi* can serve as analytical headings by means of which we can describe the content of rhetoric dealing with failure. At one and the same time the *topoi* identify ways of understanding failures, ways of talking about our understandings, and analytic headings that are commonly available to people who must deal with failure. These headings are critically useful to describe and evaluate such rhetorical responses.

Another way to think of the *topoi* is to conceive what needs to be accomplished in dealing with any instance of failure. I have argued that any failure must be therapeutically treated rhetorically by (1) providing a definition of the failure, (2) assigning fault or blame for the failure, and (3) pointing to options for repairing the failure. Consolation and compensation entail these functions. One can readily see that all three functions are interrelated. Failures will be defined in such ways that fault can be assigned, and they will be defined in ways that give rise to options for repair. The assignment of fault and responsibility will depend on how the failure has been defined, and very often the assignment automatically points to options for repair, as when the guilty are fittingly punished.

The available options for repairing a failure can, of course, dictate the definition of the problem and the assignment of fault. Our understanding of problems is often made to fit a prevailing or favored theory of problems in general. We often blame those whom we desire to blame or who are available to blame. This is the logic of the "scapegoat," and such reasoning is common to people's attempts to make failure intelligible and manageable. The point is that the definition of failure, the interpretation of fault, and the formation of remedial response are all strategic and inherently rhetorical in managing failure.

THE *TOPOI* OF FAILURE

I have said that the *topoi* are dialectical terms, and the ways of understanding and expressing failure drawn from these *topoi* place failure in a field of discussion that is first and foremost humanly meaningful and, second, strategically efficacious. That is, there are good reasons why failures, faults, and solutions must be individual or collective, past or potential, pragmatic or ideal. At least in Western culture, there are no general answers to "What is the matter?" "Who or what is to blame?" and "What is to be done?" that cannot be seen to employ these *topoi* implicitly or explicitly.

In chapter 2 I argued that our definitions of failure are fundamentally bound up with questions of personal and collective identity. This is logically so, since failure requires someone fail, that someone be at fault, and that some solution involving human response be found. I noted that the *topoi* are also typical areas of response to what Baumeister summarizes as the basic questions about identity: "How shall I relate to others?" "What shall I strive to become?" and "How will I make the basic decisions needed to guide life?" The *topoi* are not exclusive to discussions of failure, but they are always germane to discussing the relationships between an identity and its salient involvements with the world, relationships wherein failure may occur or be located by definitions and interpretations. To call something a failure and address that failure rhetorically is to give the experience a meaning and significance that have consequences for human identity.

A failure and a fault must be personal or collective. They relate to something done or projected. Failures and faults are problems born of human involvement with ideas, attitudes, and material actions. Further, to associate a failure with personal identification or involvement is necessarily to value that involvement—else "failure" as an interpretation would not be possible. Each side of each *topos*—self or society, past or future, spiritual or material—can be either positively or negatively valued, and the sides of each pair can be set rhetorically in direct opposition to one another. How one side or another is valued depends upon the specific content a person associates with it and on how that content is treated in relation to persons, institutions, and values. That is not the case with all of the pairs or notions out of which we build claims and arguments. Cause–effect relations, for instance, or large–small comparisons, or mass–weight ratios do not in and of themselves give rise to evaluative positions. But self in relation to society, past in relation to future, and spiritual in relation to material cannot be discussed without considerations of relative value.

Other dialectical pairs may be used in making specific arguments about a failure. One might discuss feasibility–infeasibility, expediency–inexpediency, or strength–weakness as characteristics of a failure. But these themes are not inherent in therapeutic rhetoric because they do not necessarily involve human identity, nor are they valuational opposites in our culture. They may, of course, be given valuational connotations, but that will be done by using the therapeutic *topoi* in contexts of failure. If someone is charged with failure because he or she produced too little of something, the relative value of large–small will have to be related to some personal or social measure of quantity, to qualitative past or future experience with the quantity in question, or to spiritual-material dimensions of the quantity. Theodore Roosevelt quickly insinuated judgments about self–society through consideration of size in his famous speech "The Man with the Muck-Rake." Using claims drawn from self–society, he was able to say what failure is and where fault lies:

> It is important to this people to grapple with the problems connected with the amassing of enormous fortunes, and the use of those fortunes, both corporate and individual, in business. We should discriminate in the sharpest way between fortunes well won and fortunes ill won; between those gained in evil fashion by keeping just within the limits of mere law-honesty.

Bigness and smallness are not faults per se, but they can become faults if those qualities are acquired by disregarding social goods. Notice how these assignments of self–social values are also made in reference to spiritual–material considerations and, implicitly, in terms of past practice and expectations about future consequences. In some fashion any rhetoric that deals with failure will introduce claims and characterizations that are associated with one or more of the topical pairs I have identified.

These *topoi* are used to construct the rhetorical schemes of consolation and compensation. The *topoi* indicate both logical and stylistic formulas that can be used to persuade about any failure. The point I would emphasize here is that the logical formulas of the *topoi* and the stylistic strategies they suggest are pragmatically related ways of rendering failures humanly manageable. These *topoi* are distinctive in suggesting ways of thinking about, and of expressing interpretations of, human identity in relation to existential conditions.

In claims and characterizations drawn from these *topoi,* one can observe the interpretation of existential conditions in pragmatically propitious ways. How does one console except by pointing to some social dimension of the situation? One may say that social elements, not individual faults, caused the failure; that social gains accrue as a result of the individual loss; that such failures are part of social history, and, as social life is inevitable, are thus fated. When we console, we put failure in the past. We define past causes and precedents; we may see that past conditions fated us to fail and that we could not have done otherwise. To accomplish this interpretation, we reorganize and reinterpret that past so as to explain the causes and minimize the effects of the failure. Thinking in this way, we may come to see the entire history of human failures as a consolation for the specific failure we now suffer (recall Demosthenes' line). When consoling we can also turn to the spiritual side of life, see the spiritual gains of learning, growth, and sacrifice that are obtained through failure. In King's basically religious formula we see material suffering called spiritually redemptive. We can then understand loss as part of God's will or part of some spiritual equation. Spiritual meanings can then be offered and accepted as substitutes for the success we had originally intended. Both "society" and "the past" are frequently infused with spiritual meaning as we look for categories of enduring or transcendent meaning to console us for temporal, ephemeral, immanent losses.

Rhetoric aiming at compensation seeks in some measure to minimize or erase failure, to set things right without significant loss. Instead of providing interpretive grounds from which one can transcend failure, the goal of compensatory interpretation is to transform failure into some alternative success. Here the individual rather than society is the focus of one's interpretations. One tries to redefine the situation so that the self is not at fault, so that self is not seriously damaged nor stained. Individual interests and prospects are sustained despite failure, and one can continue to pursue success. Compensation involves emphasizing the future.

56

It is in the future that possibility and opportunity for success exist, and one seeks to define the future as one where the failures and losses of the past will not affect the attainment of goals. As long as the future can be realistically pictured as one allowing success, failure is minimized, and can perhaps be erased by time and effort. In compensation, material considerations become especially important. While spiritual fault may be identified in a definition of a failure, material prospects can be portrayed as undamaged. With such an interpretation, the spiritual loss is made less important than the prospect for success.

Two final points need to be made about the *topoi* as they are used to deal with failure. First, the lines of thought and expression that yield consolation do not preclude additional lines of thought that promise compensation. The pairs of *topoi* are dialectical, not merely oppositional. This was adequately illustrated by the King speech.

A second point about the *topoi* is that they are related to dualisms that are maintained in our standard interpretations of existential circumstances so that self–society, past–future, and spiritual–material become acknowledged as legitimate and meaningful ways of composing such dialectical strategies. They are available interpretations to use for understanding and communicating when failure occurs. The three pairs of *topoi* I have identified are not used exclusively to cope with failure; but resort to these *topoi* is inevitable when one seeks rhetorical ways of defining, interpreting, and resolving senses of failure. They are *topoi* of human identity and its meaningful relations to the world. Any assertion of failure will force us to examine what there is to say about the self–society, past–future, and spiritual–material relationships of people and their situations. These themes give us an essential language with which to talk effectively about failure.

I have tried to show how consolation and compensation and the *topoi* speak to the needs and requirements of the individual who must manage identity rhetorically. Proponents of world views, religions, and other all-encompassing points of view treat the universal problem of human failure and propose universal solutions, or at least universal therapeutic logics whereby problems may be understood and resolved. As William James and Eric Hoffer pointed out, embracing views of the world also speak to individual needs, although they may do so in collective and universal terms. The three pairs of *topoi* are primary resources for dealing with the human issues surrounding the existence of failure. They are used in composing general or universal analyses of and responses to failure. This is logical because they help to make failure intelligible to individuals and to empower individuals to respond effectively.

To summarize, the theory of coping with failure that I propose asserts the following: We respond to failure by using symbolic resources through which we construct remedies to failure. We may produce these responses as intrapersonal, interpersonal, political, or metaphysical rhetoric. Regardless of which of these formats is used, the symbolic processes will be therapeutic in rationale, and the functions and operational strategies will be essentially the same. A complete response to a sense of failure usually requires that both consolation and compensation be accomplished or that the potential for accomplishing both be implied in the position taken. Accordingly, the rhetoric involved will have certain predictable features. It will define and reconstruct perceptions of the failure; its development will make use of themes drawn from the three pairs of *topoi;* and it will enable the individual to make the dialectical changes of view that are required in managing failure. These features of the rhetoric are necessary because the basic relationships of identity to a world where failure can occur must be altered in ways suggested by the *topoi* I have identified. In the following chapters I will exemplify and amplify these propositions about therapeutic rhetoric.

4

FAILURE AND SOCIAL DOMINION

The *topos* self–society is certainly not a new theme in considering human error. The Greeks surely had a sense of society in which the individual participated, and scholars have observed a gradual emergence of notions of personal responsibility and individuality in Greek drama and ethics. Concern for self has developed as a theme through Christian and philosophical thought, and themes of social concern have variously developed in different times and situations. There have also been different treatments of self–society cooperation and conflict. In Machiavelli's attempt to reform the rhetoric of monarchy, in Martin Luther's reformation of individual relations with God, in American revolutionary rhetoric, and in the federal Constitution, the themes of individualism and individual–social compromise were prominent. As I pointed out in chapter 2, however, in contemporary rhetoric dealing with failure the *topos* of self–society seems especially pervasive.

The dialectic of self and society informs virtually all modern psychological and social thought. Attempts to reform the self–society relationship as a way of resolving failure can be observed in Freudian and Marxist theories and their applications, in the literature of alienation and existentialism, and in the rhetoric of nearly all reformist movements from the Nazis to the Moral Majority. At some point each of these doctrines and movements identifies division between self and society as a prominent cause of failure and as a problem at which resolutions must be aimed.

There is a vast amount of rhetoric that treats the problems of the individual in society. Whether it be Thoreau or Marx, Hitler or Roosevelt, it is common for the failures that an author experiences or observes to become the grounds for some program of reform. About such cases I think it significant that each program of social reform requires that the individual implement necessary social changes by altering his or her identity. Even those, such as the existentialists, who conceive society to be the cause of all individual failing come to see changes in the identity of the individual as necessary to therapeutic resolution to failures. However self and society are defined, and whether fault is ultimately conceived as social or individual, solutions for failure require that self and society somehow be reunited. The nature of responsibility for error thus involves the individual and his or her identity in accommodating change. Regardless of where fault lies, the individual must be responsive in order to effect change. The arguments drawn from the self–society *topos* must, then, somehow relate individual identity to society in a direct, substantive way.

The functioning of the self–society *topos* can be illustrated by examining rhetoric that places blame on the individual for society's failures. This discourse appears in exhortations by contemporary authors who urge that society adapt to radically changing circumstances. To resolve the failures that they see, these authors allege that individuals must manifest major changes in their identities and value orientations. In their efforts to effect change in society, these authors use arguments wherein the fault or blame for failure is seen as caused by individual identity. They seem literally to "discover" a rhetorical need for the self–society *topos,* and the consequences of their uses of the *topos* have a dramatic impact on their rhetoric.

When the self–society *topos* is resorted to in rhetoric, an ideal relationship between the two entities is implicitly or explicitly posited. The failure is seen as a result of some violation of the ideal relationship between self and society. The resolution must be a consolation or compensation that invokes or achieves that ideal relationship. This is hardly an eccentric pattern of thinking. The traditional Western ideal has a social order in which individuals and their interests are so integrated in and supported by society that harmony and cooperation are sustained. In this ideal, society is an extension of individuals and a means for mutual benefit.

There is another ideal, however, from which people have argued and sometimes argue today. This ideal places a special value on society, and it posits that the social order should be harmonious with the order of nature. Typically, it is argued that individuals should conform to social order to ensure the survival of society. Individuals must do this, not so much for their own benefit (although ultimately this too is argued), but because they are responsible for the continued survival of society and its moral propriety. Such rhetoric urges that society and its success or value are the measures of individual action and worth. Failures are then viewed as caused by individuals who violate or neglect to observe social priorities.

This particular formulation of the self–society *topos* is familiar in traditional religious and social thought. It involves a picture of the world where the individual is ultimately responsible. It is somewhat surprising that this formulation is also at the heart of contemporary scientific rhetoric that urges society and individuals to adapt to natural conditions in order to survive.

Many contemporary authors arm themselves with scientific knowledge about the natural environment and use the "certainty" of scientific knowledge to set standards for what society should and must be. In the abstract it is not a moral propriety that is sought, as in religious rhetoric, but in arguing that individuals can and should change themselves to redeem society the arguments come to be moral arguments. Much contemporary scientific rhetoric focuses on adaptation as the means of social survival. Science gives us knowledge of physical laws and natural conditions, and these laws and conditions are taken to be standards to which society and hence individual identities must adapt. The patterns of thought this reflects are not new. W. K. C. Guthrie has noted that "concentration on the necessity of adaptations to conditions" was featured in pre–Socratic Greece and in seventeenth-century England, as it is in the West today. Physicalistic theories (such as evolution) are offered as the basis for social truths.[1] Guthrie believes that where the "natural" legitimacy of social mores is challenged and ethics are seen as matters of convention, expediency and interest are primary motivations. Where there is ethical relativity and sophistic values, society and moral standards are treated as adaptations to circumstances rather than as spiritually grounded. Under such conditions, circumstances are the rhetorical grounds for motivating changes in social standards and in individual behavior.

I recently observed a clear example of such adaptive rhetoric in an article on "Faculty Stress." The essay reported that many academics experience a great deal of stress, the cause of which can be attributed to various aspects of the university environment and to faculty roles. The essay listed major symptoms of such stress and then listed various solutions that faculty members may employ. The solutions amounted to a set of changes that faculty members should make in identity, behavior, and life style. These therapeutic solutions were coping strategies. They did not involve changing the social conditions that cause stress, nor did they include eliminating stress in any way. The therapy offered took the form of adaption by eradicating (compensating for) the effects of stress on one's health and happiness. "Stress," both here and generally, is cast in the rhetoric of "disease," diagnosed as a medical problem, and conceived of as a physical cause of problems one cannot change and so must adapt to. Clearly the essay intended to provide ways of compensating for stress in one's life. But when stress is presented as an inevitable and unchangeable condition, the entire attitude recommended toward stress might yield consolation. The rhetoric promised individual, material, and future values, but it implicitly assumed that the past, social, and spiritual causes of stress in university policies are priorities that either should not or cannot be changed to reduce stressful conditions of employment.

The incidental essay on stress illustrates the rhetorical pattern followed by a number of contemporary authors who proclaim that conditions are desperate, and that huge social and ecological problems threaten human survival. Such authors rely on scientific "knowledge" to forecast the "inevitable," to which humans must adapt. The conditions identified are given highest priority by being treated as certain and inevitable.

This rhetoric, like that of the stress essay, intends to persuade us toward compensations that derive from adapting to inescapable conditions. Individuals will have to undergo changes and make adaptations. Also like the stress essay, however, this rhetoric may be more consoling than compensating. Defining problems as inevitable, huge, and foreboding, and diagnosing individual miseries as caused by such problems consoles people for their suffering.

This is the general rhetorical pattern followed by four contemporary publicists whose rhetoric I propose to examine in detail. All emphasize that proper adaptation to certain inescapable forces requires changes in individuals' identities. The discourse of Paul Ehrlich, Alvin Toffler, B. F. Skinner, and Jeremy Rifkin illustrates this contemporary way of developing self–society themes. This quartet of writers and a good many other scientistic thinkers offer what could be called modern-day apocalyptic discourse. The visions of future conditions these seers reveal to us are endowed with scientific legitimacy. Science reveals what is necessary for survival. Science is thus represented as a kind of all-encompassing, spiritual way of understanding and determining nature and priorities. Changes must come despite individual, material prospects. As do religious apocalyptics, these reformers argue from the presumed ends and towards conclusions about what individuals must do and be. Also like religious apocalyptics, these scientistic reformers seek not only changes in present actions; they also seek to produce identities that will be adaptable whenever conflicts between self and society arise. That is, they seek a permanent solution to failures caused by improper adaptation, and the change involves a fundamental change of individual identity. While religious reformers use apocalyptic prophecies to convert sinners and forge

62

proper followers, these scientistic reformers seek to produce future selves that will adapt by changing whenever social needs come into conflict with individual interests.

FAILURE AND FUTURISM

If, as Guthrie notes, there are times when physical laws come to replace religious and societal doctrines as the legitimizing grounds of ethics and behavior, then it is perhaps also true that at such times scientific prediction comes to replace religious prophecy. The revelations of science can support the apocalyptic rhetoric that urges us to conform to some higher law before it is too late. Such rhetoric argues that there is or must be a schism between past traditions and future actions. Ultimately the rhetors reunify the future ideal with some Edenic idea or goal derived from the past. This rhetoric argues that there is such a vast gulf between spiritual ideals and material circumstances that either spiritual goals must be transformed or material actions must change in order to realign material reality with spiritual good. What this rhetoric does with the self–society relationship in order to assign responsibility and motivate changes of identity tends to be accomplished by using traditional strategies drawn from the *topos* self–society.

Using "hard" scientific data about population trends, Paul Ehrlich is at once the most strictly scientific and the most dramatically apocalyptic of the four authors I will examine. In the early 1970s, he began the zero population growth movement with his book *The Population Bomb.*[2] Ehrlich's titles display his penchant for the dramatic. His most recent work argues the likelihood of *Extinction!*[3] The 1969 essay "Eco–Catastrophe!" reveals Ehrlich's apocalyptic format in condensed form.[4] There he describes disease and famine sweeping the globe after the death of the earth's oceans. Ultimately all life on our planet is destroyed. Ehrlich's scenario of the future is retrospective, a fictional history written as though it were 1979, recalling the disastrous incidents of the previous ten years. This backward-looking perspective helps Ehrlich to certify that his prophecy is indeed certain if something is not done immediately.

Similar dramatic flair and apocalyptic style are present in Alvin Toffler's *Future Shock,* now a classic of the futurist genre. Like Ehrlich, Toffler wrote a scenario of a disastrous near future, describing how then present trends (1970) will impact the world. Toffler argued that the rate of change in society is very like a natural phenomenon, a kind of physical law of acceleration that destroys the stability of society and tradition. To combat this enemy, Toffler offers a "broad new theory of adaptation," believing that "unless man quickly learns to control the rate of change in his personal affairs as well as society at large, we are doomed to a massive adaptational breakdown."[5] The solution Toffler offered came in the form of new "knowledge." His new theory of adaptation would "help us cope more effectively with both personal and social change by deepening our understanding of how men respond to it."[6]

The apocalyptic formats used by Ehrlich and Toffler are clearly intended to assault our perceptions of present circumstances as normal or tolerable and to shake our complacency about circumstances and the adaptations we make to them. Knowledge about the world is offered in these formats, but what is addressed are the self-images of the audience and their orientations toward the phenomena of the world. It is not individual actions per se that have brought about impending peril but certain individual and collective viewpoints have led to dangerous actions. Fault is diagnosed as lying in people's identities; and while changes in actions and practices must occur, people must first alter their expectations and sense of security. They must change their identities and thereby change the society that is based on those identities. These authors want their audiences to internalize views of the future, making those views motivating world views. Only when the recommended views and principles are accepted as frameworks for choice and action will humans be able to make the kinds of adaptations needed for survival. That is the nature of the adaptation called for in the rhetoric of Ehrlich and Toffler.

The laws or principles that must be internalized here are offered as "scientific," and thus are interpreted as certain and credible ways of knowing the future and diagnosing the present. These arguments are aimed at producing an attitudinal response in audiences. Readers' minds must change before any solution to problems can be found. The rhetorical devices for achieving this response are directed toward how people presently see the self–society relationship and how they can be made to see it differently. In short, Ehrlich and Toffler seek a way to make people internalize responsibility for effects of overwhelming and impersonal laws that cause human failure.

When discussing the rhetorical nature of guilt in chapter 2, I noted Robert Lifton's perspective on guilt as the "broken connection" between people and the environment. In his work with the survivors of Japan's nuclear holocaust, Lifton observed what he called an "animating guilt" that motivated survivors to work against the "cause" of their suffering. He noted that guilt was experienced as a result of the disintegration of these people's environment, and that guilt was presented or experienced as the "psychological equivalents of death."[7] It appears that people find ways of being responsible for impersonal catastrophe as a means to adapt to and cope with their situations. They internalize the causes of the catastrophe as part of their basic identities and frameworks for responding. This is what Ehrlich and Toffler ask their readers to do.

Rhetorical imagery that amounts to "psychological equivalents of death" abounds in the prose of Ehrlich and Toffler. Ehrlich gives us a grim view of mass famine and overcrowding on a "moribund globe." The ocean, symbol of life and its origins, is pronounced dead. The ultimate catastrophe is pictured, and Ehrlich gives his reader a new vocabulary of death: "ecosystem destabilization," "red-tides," and "Thanodrin poisoning" are the new killers. Toffler resorts to similar imagery in his vocabulary of death: change is a "disease," and later a "firestorm" which "spawns in its wake all sorts of curious social flora—from psychedelic churches and 'free universities' to science cities in the Artic and wife-swap clubs in California."[8] It is interesting from a contemporary perspective to notice that the symptoms of "disease" that Toffler cites are all phenomena that unsettled people in the late 1960s.

From diverse concrete experiences of the audience in their present, Toffler brought forth a common diagnosis of "change," introduced as the "death of permanence." He wrote:

> Millions of human beings will find themselves increasingly disoriented, progressively incompetent to deal rationally with their environments. The malaise, mass neurosis, irrationality, and free-floating violence already apparent in contemporary life are merely a foretaste of what may lie ahead unless we come to understand and treat this disease.[9]

Clearly Toffler's rhetoric urged readers to be "shocked," not only at this possible future, but at those elements in their present lives that this interpretation of the future threw into relief.

Toffler actually gave his audience a rhetorical version of shock therapy, his book treating the kinds of maladies and malaise readers then suffered. This is the kind of therapy Kenneth Burke noted in inspirational literature; therapy that is performed while one is reading the book. The various ailments of modern social life, too disparate or fragmented to be understood as a single problem, are named and cast out as the demon "change." The remedy for these ailments is willingness to adapt to change; the procedures amount to little more than buying Toffler's "broad new theory of adaptation"; that is, acquiring some understanding of the disease and accepting its inevitability. Toffler's use of the disease metaphor reveals the medicinal logic of his therapy. What at the beginning of his book is a "disease" that "invades" from without is, by the end of the book, a "cancer," a "wild growth" that comes from the inside. The cure for this disease is to internalize it as part of the self, and that is what his theory of adaptation is intended to help us do.

The medical analogy can be carried even further in describing Toffler's therapy. The book is rather like an inoculation of future shock given to patient-readers. A rhetorically controlled dose of the disease seems intended to make readers marshal their defenses and so become better able to withstand the disease in the future. This therapeutic pattern is also very much like demonology as described by Rollo May: "The one way to get over daimonic possession is to possess *it,* by frankly confronting it, coming to terms with it, integrating it into the self system."[10] Toffler's words echo this pattern:

> The individual who has internalized the principle of acceleration—who understands in his bones as well as his brain that things are moving faster in the world around him—makes an automatic, unconscious compensation for the compression of time. Anticipating that situations will endure less long, he is less frequently caught off guard and jolted than the person whose durational expectancies are frozen.[11]

Like the daimonic possession of self that May analyzes, the demon of change must come to be understood as part of the self—internalized, integrated, and thus brought under control.

The goal here, and in Ehrlich's rhetoric, seems to be to make the experience of reading sufficiently strong that a reader's attitudinal responses are shaped. Are there really *actions* that are sought as a result of the rhetoric? In Ehrlich's scheme there was at least the possibility of some kinds of action that might remedy the ecological problem. He focused specifically on the population problem, and ultimately his rhetoric sought to cause people to restrict their families, to have different expectations about procreation, and simply to *be* the kind of people who did not have large families. For Toffler the specified remedy seems to be purely attitudinal; one must simply "unfreeze" one's expectations about the future. But that would seem to require a "freezing" of that portion of one's self that leads to such expectations. One's sense of and desire for permanence must "die," and this is a death that Toffler, like Ehrlich, pronounces inevitable. All that is left is for people to adapt to the "facts" by restricting self and making self essentially more adaptable.

I began this investigation with the hope of learning more about the role of the self–society *topos* in treating failure. These two apocalyptic writers deal with what they consider enormous human failures. Their rhetoric identifies causes of failure, but there is really little that solves those problems. The problems were presented as insoluble precisely to achieve the shock effects the authors seek. Solving the problems would require revolution and massive overhaul of institutions and behaviors, something beyond either the wishes or the capabilities of the authors. Coping with these problems, however, by making adjustments in beliefs and expectations is a rhetorically legitimate possibility. I am concerned with the ways of coping that are presented. They appear to be ways of mass compensation for problems as defined; but given those problems, they are really perspectives and knowledge that are consoling for losses suffered in the readers' lives and futures.

In the works of Ehrlich and Toffler there is little discussion of society in and of itself, or of the individual. Where, then, is the relationship of self–society? The spiritual character of self and society is treated only in terms of its necessary adaptation to the material circumstances of self and society. Our spiritual fault is not in goals or traditions that otherwise might be noble, but only in our inadequate knowledge of material circumstances and our lack of a scientific attitude toward adapting to those circumstances. Failure then lies in a gap between spiritual being and its integration with material circumstances. Failure threatens because of the immense gulf between the expectations of the past and those of the future. But failure can be solved by the individual's submission to the priorities of society. That is, individuals must internalize responsibility for what all of society is doing in its maladjustment to the material environment. Where society has failed, the individual must make compensation. For what the individual loses, survival and the well-being of society offer consolation.

In the problems of overpopulation or accelerated change, society would seem to be implicated since it is social practices that sustain the problems. Toffler points blame at "technocratic society" and at society's failure to educate individuals to the problem of change. In both cases, however, there also is an implied indictment of the individualism that society sustains, and the kinds of rights, expectations, and services that individuals demand from the world. Society as such is never really assailed; the responsibility for both the causes and effects of the problems is placed with the individual. However, it appears that the "good" brought about by individual change is not primarily, or purely, a social good. The real good appears to be to make the individual serve some kind of higher social order for the good of humankind, hence for the good of the individual.

Ehrlich and Toffler illustrate how vaguely experienced ills and anxieties can be rhetorically forged into a broad definition of failure. The individual failures of an audience can be used as evidence for the definition and diagnosis of the failure that the author favors. In this sense, the diagnosis of such failures is in itself consolatory, allowing the individual to heap frustrations into an objectifiable pile. The enumeration of miseries and the apocalyptic prophecy exacerbate the audience's awareness of its troubles and makes the desire for explanations and solutions stronger.

When Ehrlich and Toffler deal with the next step, the cure is not remediation of the now defined problem. Their cures come about when each individual internalizes the problem as defined. The move does not involve dealing with aspects of the problem that are outside the self—for example, some problem with society's structure. The strategy used by Ehrlich and Toffler is to treat the broadly defined failure as one that requires personal adaptation. The procedure is akin to that which Kenneth Burke calls "mortification," where the rhetoric urges a "slaying of the self" to set social order right again.[12] Social problems are solved by individuals' acts of purification, without challenging the fact or principle that society holds priority over the self.

The audiences already possessed the therapeutic procedures for dealing with such conflicts and crises as Ehrlich and Toffler portrayed. If Burke's analysis of mortification has merit, the audiences understood from their general Judeo-Christian heritage that society can be purified of fault (and freed from wrath) through individuals' mortification and self-diminishment. Ehrlich and Toffler told their audiences such personal diminishment was "the right thing to do" in the face of cataclysm. This is not the only way impending catastrophe can be handled rhetorically, but it is a viable option. In both secular and religious rhetoric there is a genuine and even expected pattern of dealing with self–society themes in ways that dictate submissive self-change. This is widely taken as an intelligible and legitimate way of remedying failure—especially those failures that individuals have difficulty identifying and understanding until given some simplifying, organizing "law" that explains all. B. F. Skinner, it seems to me, worked out a veritable technology for mortification and he did so with the same scientific focus on adaptation that was fundamental to the arguments of Ehrlich and Toffler.

A TECHNOLOGY FOR MORTIFICATION

B. F. Skinner's *Beyond Freedom and Dignity* is another illustration of scientific apocalyptic. Like Ehrlich, Skinner saw the state of society and its relationship to the natural world as requiring radical behavioral reform. Like Toffler, Skinner saw the necessary changes as requiring a new theory of human behavior and motivation. Skinner's theoretical rhetoric was concerned with supplying ways and means of producing adaptation to the environment. His analysis was intended to show how society must change to make individuals more adaptable; however the rhetorical requirements of this move involved offering individual change as a way of producing necessary social change. Skinner wished for a society that is technologically capable of producing individual changes, but to achieve this he must persuade individuals that they should relinquish individuality and willfully perform a massive adaptation (compensation) for the sake of future social survival. In short, Skinner addressed the relationship of self to society, and in this relationship he found the locus of both individual and social failure.

Skinner's introductory comments display the same apocalyptic strategies employed by Ehrlich and Toffler:

> But things grow steadily worse, and it is disheartening to find that technology itself is increasingly at fault. Sanitation and medicine have made the problems of population more acute, war has acquired a new horror with the invention of nuclear weapons, and the affluent pursuit of happiness is largely responsible for pollution. As Darlington has said, "Every new source from which man has increased his power on the earth has been used to diminish the prospects of his successors. All of his progress has been made at the expense of damage to his environment which he cannot repair and could not foresee."
>
> Whether or not he could have foreseen the damage, man must repair it or all is lost. And he can do so only if he recognizes the nature of the difficulty.[13]

Once again the solution to present problems is defined as a new understanding. This implies that the failure is again a failure of knowledge and the solution is better knowledge. Once more this saving knowledge is drawn from science.

What is needed, according to Skinner, is the kind of power over people that scientists have acquired over the material environment. Skinner said that a "technology of behavior comparable in power and precision to

69

physical and biological technology is lacking." He noted that the idea of a behavioral technology encounters ideological resistance: "Those who do not find the very possibility ridiculous are more likely to be frightened by it than reassured."[14] Skinner answered by assaulting the attitude behind this resistance, repeating his apocalyptic warning that this is "how far we are from preventing the catastrophe toward which the world seems to be inexorably moving."

Skinner's analysis of the problem quickly focused on the relationships of the individual and society, and he located failure in the value Western culture places on individualism. What must be altered to cure the problem is the relative priority of self and society; individuals must be motivated to work for the success and survival of society. Skinner defined the problem as an ideological one, realizing that this task was rhetorical. He must motivate individuals by drawing upon some concept of individual responsibility consistent with their orientations to self–society–environment relationships.

To redefine the audience's conception of responsibility, Skinner attacked the grounds of praise and blame in contemporary society and proposed new grounds for evaluation:

> Freedom and dignity illustrate the difficulty. They are the possessions of the autonomous man of traditional theory, and they are essential to practices in which a person is held responsible for his conduct and given credit for his achievements. A scientific analysis shifts both the responsibility and the achievement to the environment.[15]

Here Skinner observed that being responsible for one's failures is tied to the possibilities of individual success, and he recognized that both are vital underpinnings of individual identity. To vanquish individual identity would require that all perception of individual failures, responsibility, and success be transformed. Skinner's rhetorical solution was to abolish individualistic virtues, such as "freedom and dignity." He proposed a new relationship based upon social priorities and values.

Skinner addressed the self–society relationship straightforwardly. The conflict or problem was between self and society, and the solution specified that self should be devalued and society given greater value. Skinner directly sought to make social science emulate physical science. As in the rhetoric of Ehrlich and Toffler, Skinner's rhetoric made science coequal with environment. The same power and inevitability that the physical sciences attribute to environment was imparted to society. Like other organisms that must adapt to the environment in order to survive, people must adapt to society with like priorities and with eagerness for self-change. As Skinner argued the case, the idea of individual control over the environment would be removed from the vocabulary and replaced with an idea of social control. In his analysis power and control lie within a "species" or "cultural" identity. Only when people forsake their individual identities and participate in a collective identity can they gain control. Skinner rationalized that even though "man himself may be controlled by his environment, it is an environment almost wholly of his own making." For this dictum to be consoling, social control of environment must be assigned first priority and "autonomous man" duly humbled.

The claim that science and technology really can control the material environment is startling. It is precisely a lack of such control that would seem to be to blame for the social predicament Skinner describes as "inexorable catastrophe." However, Skinner adopted the position that in their social dimension, science and technology are pure; failure has come from their service to individual values.

Skinner thus exalted social identity and in it found the promise of control. In Skinner's society the individual must be mortified, and Skinner's rhetoric attempts to engender an attitude of mortification. He explained:

> The individual nevertheless remains merely a stage in a process which began long before he came into existence and will long outlast him. He has no ultimate responsibility for a species trait or cultural practice, even though it was he who underwent the mutation or introduced the practice which became part of the species or culture.[16]

One must compensate for mistaken identity by sacrificing individual achievement, but Skinner's vision offered consolation by making the individual part of a process larger than the self. We become part of something that transcends individual success and failure. Sacrifice of the individual allows the spiritual and material to be united and the past and future to be merged in eternity—all through the social element of human identity.

The shift of perception required to bring about this revolution in human identity is, of course, radical. Skinner said that "a person does not act upon the world, the world acts upon him."[17] Our basic relationship to the world must then be purified of the idea that individuals influence the environment. Skinner would suppress the very vocabulary of individual worth—a rhetorical shift. Concepts such as "freedom," "dignity," "responsibility," "achievement," "punishment," and "credit," would be eschewed. In Skinner's analysis they are the source of our problem. They imply individual success and failure, but if control and influence are defined as external to the individual, failure will be erased and successful adaptation made possible. Concepts of individual motivation must be supplanted with scientifically formulated motivations.

Despite these strictures, individual failure is not wholly eliminated in Skinner's analysis. Individuals are expected to feel responsibility for complying with the social good. For Skinner's social rhetoric to operate, there must be some basis for a scale of values. When he discusses values, this basis becomes clear:

> [In the traditional view] a person's behavior is at least to some extent his own achievement. He is free to deliberate, decide, act, possibly in original ways, and he is to be given credit for his successes and blamed for his failures. In the scientific view . . . a person's behavior is determined by a genetic endowment traceable to the evolutionary history of the species and by the environmental circumstances to which as an individual he has been exposed. Neither view can be proved, but it is in the nature of scientific inquiry that the evidence should shift in favor of the second.[18]

Skinner appears to have defined away individual success, but not individual failure. His scientific values institutionalize individual failure.

The first value one finds by adopting this "scientific view" is that the social order will fulfill the dictates of scientific metaphysics. Individualism is not compatible with the scientific view; to hold to it is failure. Second, the new view legitimizes scientific enterprise as the overarching social goal—the value of which Skinner takes as self-evident. Not to applaud, support, or participate in scientific enterprise is presumably to fail. A third value in Skinner's system is that when people mortify individualism and display the scientific ethos of their social identity, they become open to social persuasion that is charged with "scientific values." Skinner argued that the scientific view has a "marked advantage when we begin to do something about behavior," because "autonomous man is not easily changed."[19] In short, his theory of motivation legitimizes the kinds of persuasion that are to be used, and to embrace his theory makes humans more persuadable by the techniques of that persuasion.

The circularity illustrates what I have been trying to demonstrate about therapeutic rhetoric generally: Therapeutic theories are often con-

72

structed to justify the methods of persuasion used to perform therapy. Therapies are not necessarily scientific or legitimate attempts to describe the world or self as they "really" are. Nonetheless, as in Skinner's case, the success of such theories in performing therapy is often taken as proof for the truth of the theory about what is. It is possible, however, that any number of other therapies and theories could achieve the same result.

I am suggesting that Skinner seeks a more effective kind of institutionalized persuasion in order to ensure social order. The criteria for success are cast as the requirements for successful adaptation. Adaptation can be implemented by altering the basic rhetorical patterns for evaluation of actions and motives. Ironically, this is the same kind of rhetorical pattern that Burke saw at the base of institutionalized rhetoric in religion. One seeks to "persuade men toward certain acts" by creating the "kinds of attitudes which lead to such acts."[20] The theory of world and self that underpins religious persuasion is based upon axiological assumptions about human character and its relationship to the environment. Religion inculcates these assumptions with stories of origins and endings that locate the individual in the world. Procedures such as mortification and victimage are thus grounded in the religious world view as ways of keeping one's position in the world when error or fault occur. Skinner has shown us how science can also supply such an orientation in its theories of human origins and prophecies for the future.

Skinner noted that the questions he addressed "are concerned not with man's origins but with his destiny."[21] Yet the legitimacy of Skinner's proposals depends entirely upon the story of origins that the scientific world view embraces. Skinner advanced a theory of "cultural evolution" to support the values employed in his praising and blaming. In the scientific view "species evolution" is the *fact* about our origins, and this fact leads to assigning superior values to social identity and to diminishing values of individualism. It is at this point that Skinner's reliance on the adaptation principle is most clear:

A culture, like a species, is selected by its adaptation to an environment: to the extent that it helps its members to get what they need and avoid what is dangerous, it helps them to survive and transmit the culture. The two kinds of evolution are closely interwoven. . . . *The capacity to undergo the changes in behavior which make a culture possible was acquired in the evolution of the species,* and, reciprocally, the culture determines many of the biological characteristics transmitted. Many current cultures, for example, enable individuals to survive and breed who would otherwise fail to do so.[22]

The idea of cultural evolution has these rhetorical properties: (1) It legitimizes the practice of adaptation by means of a theory and implied narrative about the origins of the species. (2) It asks that we attribute the same value to the survival of the culture as we do the survival of the species. (3) It argues that the value of cultural survival is more important than the survival of any individual. In this vein Skinner argued that "the evolution of a culture introduces an additional kind of good or value. A culture which *for any reason* induces its members to work for its survival is more likely to survive," and "survival is the only value according to which a culture is eventually to be judged."[23]

A rather difficult question emerges about the nature of this value "cultural survival." Does Skinner's insistence on this transcendent human purpose grow from his preoccupation with science, which prescribes survival by adaptation as the uppermost value of the species? Or does it instead derive from a genuine concern that *our* culture, or Skinner's culture, is threatened by extinction and this is the key failure his theory seeks to mitigate? One needs to ask *which* culture should survive. There are many "cultures" in America alone, let alone the entire human species. If *all* of these cultures were working exclusively for their own survival and working at the possible expense of others, then the possibilities of disorder seem great. As others have noted about Skinner's plan, there appears to be great potential for tyranny in its implementation.

These problems are important when we consider the rhetorical implications of Skinner's theories. First, we need to know precisely what failure is being defined and resolved. Is it failure to adapt to changing circumstances, as he says, or is it failure to preserve some past social order and its rhetorical workings? Since his psychology of adaptation so closely resembles mortification, one is invited to entertain the latter possibility. Second, Skinner wishes a "vocabulary" and "technology of behavior" that is precise, yet he has chosen culture as the embracing term and value of all social order. "Culture" is one of the least empirical, least quantifiable, and least understood concepts in the social sciences. Whoever is in charge of deciding what is in the interests of "cultural survival" and when and how individuals must adapt will be in control of the society. Even if decided democratically, which seems unworkable, these decisions would have to prescribe what failure is and how one should respond to it. That does not seem vastly different from the system Skinner seeks to replace. Finally, it would be extremely difficult to decide what successful adaptation is and is not until after such practices have either sustained or endangered part of the species. This would be especially true of physical adaptation to the environment. Controlled evolution would require total knowledge and total control, which would eliminate the accidents or inventions that have thus far enabled societies to change and survive.

The point of this criticism is that in Skinner's scheme, people are no longer being asked to adapt to situations. Instead they are being urged or conditioned to adapt to an idea. His is a therapeutic rhetoric that seeks to implement a scientific ideology as a way of making all failures of one kind, a kind of failure for which there is a technique of resolution: individual submission to a prescribed and defined social ideal. In this respect, this therapy works in ways identical with traditional Christian religion.

Skinner accepted at one point that "the parallel between biological and cultural evolution breaks down at the point of transmission. There is nothing like the chromosome-gene mechanism in the transmission of a cultural practice."[24] Rhetorical communication is the major means for transmitting cultural practices, and Skinner was implicitly searching for a more effective rhetoric to accomplish his social ideals. This is also apparent in the fact that he chose to locate our cultural problems in our vocabulary of individual values. There are methods of assuring appropriate responses to failures that, in Skinner's argot, have "evolved in the species." Religious mortification is one such method of perpetuating social order. Skinner appears to have reinvented this rhetorical technique by using a new scientific vocabulary and theory of motivation.

Like Toffler, Skinner offered a special interpretation of failure that made it seem possible to resolve the woes of contemporary diversity and disorder. Both Toffler and Skinner constructed a theory of motivation that prescribed adaptation as the means of resolving the diagnosed failure. Both theories point out how the failures of the individual in this society can be compensated by a form of personal mortification. Both authors follow typical apocalyptic strategies: they forecast inevitable doom as a way of motivating changes in the present. We are "saved," if only by the "knowledge" and "purity" of conforming to a higher law. Such complete schemes of compensation, I have noted, can serve as consolations for the suffering people experience in their present-day situations.

In Skinner's technology of mortification, all human failures are traced to the overarching cause of individualism. Individual identity must be diminished to the status of a "controlled self." Motivations of each individual must come from a controlling self, one that possesses the values of a social ideal. The division of the self into dominant and subordinate elements is, Skinner argued, "inevitable in the nature of cultural evolution. . . . When control is exercised through the design of an external environment, the selves are, with minor exceptions, distinct."[25] It appears that in a perfect state of social order individuals would permanently manifest a sense of failed or inadequate selfhood. Failure is not erased; it is institutionalized. Skinner writes that "the evolution of a culture is a gigantic exercise in self-control."[26]

A doctrinal and institutional imperative of mortification is, again, a hallmark of religious persuasion. Burke's analysis of the role of mortification in this institutionalized persuasion is borne out by Skinner's discovery of the means of persuasion. Burke argues that mortification is all-important to the institutional rhetoric of social control. It is "crucial to conditions of empire, where sacrifice and dominion come to a head."[27] Both religious rhetoric and Skinner's formulation share a common theme drawn from the self–society *topos:* self and society are placed in opposition. The rhetorical motivation of this theme is that when self comes into opposition with society, the self must undergo mortification, surrender. Failures of social order are thus repaired, and the individual is purified and rejoined with the social order. Both compensations and consolations for any failure so understood can then be achieved.

THE ORDER OF DISORDER

Toffler and Skinner both purport to offer scientific analyses of individual failures that grow from an unbalanced or inappropriate relationship between social order and natural order. Readers' senses of inadequacy, fears, and common difficulties with daily social existence are diagnosed as products of larger forces at war with individualist values and orientations. By using self–society analysis the authors identify the causes of failure with the individual and his or her values. Consolation for this failure is found in the enormity and inevitability of the forces at work and in the possibility of identification with these grand forces. Compensations are possible through mortifying responses that conform individual identity to the principles or laws of the natural order.

I have called this variety of therapeutic rhetoric apocalyptic because it follows the pattern of religious revelation. In apocalyptic religious rhetoric, interpretations of history and prophecies of the future reveal God's laws about the relationship of society and species and its implications for individual behavior. The individual must mortify to secure salvation; the truth cannot be seen or used to save the self without "faith." Toffler and Skinner's revelations are, of course, born of a different world view that science has made possible, but the structure of coping with failure is the same as in apocalyptic religious rhetoric.

The late 1970s and early 1980s were rife with such rhetoric, and some combined scientific knowledge with prophetic religious themes and language. Jeremy Rifkin's 1982 work, *Entropy: A New World View,* is an interesting example. The book proposes "new knowledge" about the physical world and our relations with it—knowledge gained from scientific inquiry. But Rifkin encases his called-for reforms in thoroughly religious formulations. He explicates the absolute law of entropy and proposes an entirely new world view.

The rhetorical features that Burke found in religious rhetoric are strikingly apparent in Rifkin's use of the concept of entropy. Burke posited that the concept of "order" is paired with an equally fundamental concept of "disorder." It is doubtful that in making this pairing Burke conceived that the physical sciences would posit disorder as the natural state of the world. Nonetheless, entropy, a postulate of the second law of thermodynamics, asserts that disorder is indeed the pattern of physical transformation in the universe, as the universe proceeds from an ordered to a disordered state of randomness. From this scientific idea, Rifkin draws his notion of ideal social order. Rifkin believes that social order must somehow adapt to the law of entropy, and this must be accomplished through changes in individual identity. To this end, his motivational rhetoric draws from the same basic themes of the self–society *topos* as those of the other authors I have considered.

Rifkin's belief that the world is "winding down" takes the scientifically legitimate idea of disorder as the natural order and infuses that notion with concepts of social order and governance. As in Skinner's rhetoric, this move makes a conceptual shift from the morally neutral concepts of physical science to moral concepts of social orientations. The shift is clear in Rifkin's use of a vocabulary of morality and religion. To take a single but fundamental instance, Rifkin introduces entropy as a "penalty" which is exacted every time energy is transformed.[28] To be *penalized* is to pay for some human failing. One would not, for example, speak of energy loss that occurs along power lines as a penalty, unless one wished to define that loss as the result of some human error or insufficiency.

It is clear that Rifkin offered his plans as a response to human failure. The failings and confusion of individuals in society are cited as evidence that the entropic principle is at work and are used as motivations for the new *understanding* that his treatment will give. *Entropy: A New World*

View was written after a decade of energy crisis, when "diminished expectations" was a common topic in political and social rhetoric. Individual prospects, values, and life styles were being threatened by gloomy forecasts of energy shortage, while people dealt day to day with the consequences of energy policy. Rifkin's scheme treats such failures by defining a fundamental and inevitable principle that explains their cause, and he offers conversions for the identities of those who suffer them. As with the other apocalyptic authors, Rifkin's new "knowledge" about the world offers a consolation in the enormity and inevitability of the problem, and offers compensations that will mitigate our perceptions of disaster.

Rifkin is not the only thinker to discover the cosmological implications of the entropy principle, nor the first to apply the principle to social order and institutions.[29] The ultimate conclusion of the entropy law is that the physical universe will decay and no longer be able to support human life—although this event may be millions of years in the future. The entropy principle necessarily diminishes the individual. It was therefore easy for Rifkin to translate this law into social and moral rules about energy consumption and waste: if work and progress accelerate extinction, then do less work; if consumption and production lead to the decay of the world, then slow them down; if there is to be less material satisfaction, then be happy with less. The old "Creation" paradigm had people doing, creating, building, and imposing the social order on the natural world. With entropy as the guiding principle, motivation is toward passivity: conform one's self-image and expectations to the truth that human accomplishments contribute to extinction, and accept that the overwhelming law of nature diminishes the importance of individual and social goals. Rifkin argued that we should form a "low-entropy culture," where we follow more "Spartan, frugal lifestyles." The new ethic would become "The less production and consumption necessary to maintain a healthy, decent life, the better."[30] In other words, the only way to deal with contemporary woes and the ultimate disintegration of the universe is to accept the causal principle as part of one's identity, to embody it in social order, and to act within the confines of this world view. This adaptive response is, again, very similar to mortification. The individual must internalize responsibility for external conditions and respond by sacrifice of self.

Burke argued that the rhetoric of religion institutionalizes certain motivations by grounding them in the "very authorship of men's motives." Thus, in religion God's act of creation grounds the creative motives whereby people build their own order and impose it on nature. In Skinner, "authorship" was grounded in a notion of cultural evolution, which he used to prescribe that society should be motivated to "evolve." In Rifkin, entropy authors the essential motivations that humans should follow in their actions. Human motivation changes from active creativity to passive conformity. However, there is still great formal similarity between the therapeutic rationales of traditional religion and Rifkin's proposals for managing failure. Even Rifkin's style and vocabulary closely resemble the style of much religious talk. He writes that "the Entropy Law has a special power. It is so utterly overwhelming that once fully internalized, it transforms everyone it comes into contact with; it is this almost mystical attraction that makes the Entropy Law so frightening to take hold of."[31] Rifkin could have interpreted the entropy principle as a motivation to fight disorder, to accelerate technological progress and scientific discovery, and to gain greater control over the material environment. Entropy might be seen as an evil to be combatted. He chose, however, to mystify entropy. It is a God-principle that ultimately reveals the only solutions to human problems. He says that

> the allure resides in its all encompassing nature. The Entropy Law is the assassin of the truths of the Modern Age, . . . truths [that] have metamorphosed into monstrous lies which threaten our continued existence. The Entropy Law is our escape to freedom, . . . unmasking and disposing of the many lies that have for so long governed the world.

With this revolution in social truth, "we experience the first ecstasy of relief that comes with being released." The mystery causes us to feel "desperately anxious, not knowing what new order the entropy paradigm will create."[32] Rifkin's proposal is an answer to these perplexities; he gives a version of "order" that responds to this new principle of disorder.

Right understanding of the world will remove perplexities and worries. Individual failures are made intelligible by the new scientific truth. By internalizing this principle and making it the social paradigm, one is liberated from the old bonds. Rifkin clearly exacerbates as he redefines the audience's perceptions of failure; this is his way of preparing them to accept his views of social order. His rhetoric calls for a complete revolution, a complete conversion of individual identities. Notice the religious tone of his counsel:

> The specifics of what is to be done can only come after a thorough cleansing away of the worst remaining vestiges of the mechanical

world view. Our own conversion is the first order of business. Only when we have cast aside forever the old way of thinking and behaving and take onto ourselves the new entropic world view will we be ready to go forth and remake our culture.[33]

Rifkin plainly calls for a purification through conversion, a radical change that evokes the dramatic language of religious conversion. "Cleansing away," "casting aside," and "going forth" are bits of familiar religious language.

Rifkin's rhetorical strategies for urging conversion are not new. He promises that conversion will fulfill the promises of spiritual pursuit:

> The traditional wisdom, as embodied in all the great world religions, has long taught that the ultimate purpose of human life is not the satisfaction of all material desires, but rather the experience of liberation that comes from becoming one with the metaphysical unity of the universe. The goal is to find "the truth that will set us free"; to find out who we really are; to identify with the Absolute Principle that binds together all of existence; to know God.[34]

The spiritual substitute for material satisfaction straightforwardly offers consolation for the sacrifices Rifkin calls for. It also can function as a consolation for the sacrifices the audience has already had to make. And the audience may need consolation for the "facts" of which they've just been apprised, that the universe will eventually dissolve and humankind will become extinct.

Rifkin becomes an apostle of scientific revelation. It is not surprising, therefore, that his rhetoric offers consolation very like that offered by religion: "It is part of God's plan." Rifkin even legitimizes this consolation by linking his paradigmatic revolution to what he calls the "Second Christian Reformation." This reformation, he alleges, is already under way in American society. He epitomizes religious rebirth as a "new stewardship doctrine." He wishes to re-form the biblical covenant between God and humanity, one that modern society, ethics, and technological progress have broken: "God, then, has a covenant with humanity. Man and women are to act as his stewards on earth, preserving and protecting all of God's creations. This covenant puts human beings in a special relationship to God."[35]

Rifkin's assertion of a "new covenant" brings to mind Burke's metaphor of social reform as "covenant-breaking and covenant-making."

Ehrlich, Toffler, and Skinner do not use this language, but the metaphor clarifies the rhetorical connotations of what they attempt. All four authors diminish individual identity as a significant force in the physical universe. Yet all four call for human participation in the governance of nature. Through individual diminishment, mortification, and restriction of action, a larger vision is revealed. Within the "reality," identity has a role and the possibility of redeeming humankind. The participation envisioned is, however, participation in knowledge, not in personal action. In Rifkin's view, humans must accept their inability to be like God in creating and directing the universe, but this understanding yields the consolation of serving a godly cause: they can function as stewards as they watch the divinely ordained plan unfold. Except that they eschew the religious vocabulary, Toffler and Skinner describe realities and prospects in ways parallel to Rifkin's. Purified selves—those who rightly understand—can participate gratifyingly in the power and authority of the principle of governance. The knowledge gained by properly suffering failure is consoling; the spiritual dimension of identity is elevated above the active, to understanding.

Rifkin's way of "preaching" is more thoroughly apocalyptic than that of the other authors I have discussed. All of the authors, however, illustrate characteristics of therapeutic rhetoric. They all treat specific failures by composing treatments in principle. Regardless of how their science or theory defines the cause of failure, all of these therapists (1) locate fault in conceptions of individual responsibility, conceptions drawn from the self–society *topos;* (2) define the fault as inadequate knowledge of or disregard for cosmological "facts" about the relationship of humanity to nature; (3) call for individuals to redefine identity by internalizing revealed facts and their implications, which involves diminishing or abandoning self and reforming identity in accordance with social requirements; (4) offer as consolation for self-diminishment the sense of a new kind of participation in a larger, true, and nature-determined scheme of things—creating harmony among the person, society, and nature.

Like traditional religious savants, these scientifically oriented rhetors ask that the self be mortified in order to achieve harmony with implacable world forces. Each offers a supernal rule of self–society relations. The scientists ground self–society relations on supernal but natural laws. In each case, the rhetorical treatment of those laws becomes increasingly supernatural with the language used to argue its force. Finally, in Rifkin, the "law" becomes completely supernatural and loses its scientific context entirely.

Ehrlich, Skinner, Toffler, and Rifkin illustrate how self–society themes are used in assimilating new knowledge and promoting identity change. They all presuppose that personal and social problems exist, and that these need remediation through the use of theoretical knowledge. While their views or projects are not typical of all scientists or popular therapists, the patterns of their analyses and reformist urgings are representative of what must be done rhetorically if one chooses to offer encompassing therapies for personal and social faults. These authors do not begin with doctrinally defined failures and doctrinally specified causes, as many ideologists do. These writers seek to inculcate new world views. They identify failure, locate the causes and consequences, diagnose the nature of the failure, and then prescribe solutions that address the problem as defined. As "scientific" reformers, they provide cosmological and theoretical bases for their appeals. Yet they rediscovered motivational relationships that are commonplaces of the self–social *topos*. From this examination, we get a view of how the self–society *topos* functions as a necessary feature of composing therapeutic rhetoric.

One reason the self–social *topos* is necessary in therapeutic rhetoric is that regardless of how external to the individual or society the cause of failure is, to motivate management of failure requires that responsibility be assigned. That is, where a response is required, those who are responsible must be found. To work within the context of contemporary self–society assignments, the authors I have studied had to assign responsibility to the individualistic orientations of the audience and to urge changes in their readers' individual identities. This is true even of Skinner, who denied the existence of individual identity. Something like guilt was evoked as these authors pictured the individual's relationship to society and the physical world. Responsibility for immediate actions was placed squarely on the individual, even when it was society that needed to be redeemed. Under this construal of self–society relations, social reform had to be accomplished in and through individual identity.

The authors examined here located the problem in individual persons, in their identities and psychological constitutions. Their rhetoric can therefore be read as a spiritual or moral protest against individualism. Ehrlich, it is true, seems ultimately to have sought actions that would compensate for problems, but the other three authors seem to have composed moral diagnoses and exhortations—a rhetorical phenomenon perhaps explained by the enormity and inexorability of the problems as the authors diagnosed them.

That these "scientific" authors communicated in ways similar to those used to invoke religious mortification suggests that the rhetorical pattern

82

has widespread applicability in therapeutic rhetoric where the *topos* of self and society furnishes the bases for persuasion.

The examples I have used do not exploit the only possible uses of self–society themes. Were we to examine rhetoric applauding individual over collective concerns we would see milder or perhaps no demands for personal mortification. For example, praise of free enterprise or of creativity will deal less with reform of self and more with reform of society, institutions, laws, and the like. A general point to be emphasized is that wherever in our society the self–society *topos* is drawn upon, the legitimacy of individualism becomes an issue. Had the scientists I examined been cognitive psychologists or followers of William James's kind of pragmatism, we would have seen uses of self–society themes that magnified the powers and dignity of the individual and perhaps diminished the relative standing of society or the physical universe. In any case, however, if self–society themes are used, individual failures will be diagnosed, blame attributed, and prescriptions that promote some kind of change will be offered. This mode of dealing with shortcomings has existed throughout the history of human communication.

NOTES

1. W. K. C. Guthrie, *The Sophists* (Cambridge: Cambridge University Press, 1971), 55–60.
2. Paul Ehrlich, *The Population Bomb* (New York: Ballantine, 1968).
3. Paul Ehrlich, *Extinction!* (New York: Random House, 1981).
4. "Eco-Catastrophe!," *The Futurists,* ed. Alvin Toffler (New York: Random House, 1972, 13–26. Originally published in *Ramparts,* Sept. 1969.
5. Alvin Toffler, *Future Shock* (New York: Random House, 1970), 4.
6. Toffler, 5.
7. Robert J. Lifton, *The Broken Connection* (New York: Simon and Schuster, 1980), 139.
8. Toffler, 4, 11.
9. Toffler, 13.
10. Rollo May, "Psychotherapy and the Daimonic," *Myths, Dreams, and Religion,* ed. Joseph Campbell (New York: Dutton, 1970), 201.
11. Toffler, 41–42.
12. Kenneth Burke, *The Rhetoric of Religion* (1961; rpt. Berkeley: University of California, 1970), 190–91.
13. B. F. Skinner, *Beyond Freedom and Dignity* (New York: Knopf, 1971), 3–4.
14. Skinner, 5.
15. Skinner, 25.
16. Skinner, 209.
17. Skinner, 211.

18. Skinner, 101.
19. Skinner, 101.
20. Burke, v.
21. Skinner, 102.
22. Skinner, 129–30; italics added.
23. Skinner, 136.
24. Skinner, 130.
25. Skinner, 206.
26. Skinner, 215.
27. Burke, 190–91.
28. Jeremy Rifkin, *Entropy: A New World View* (New York: Viking, 1980), 36.
29. See, e.g., Fritjof Capra's *The Turning Point* (New York: Simon and Schuster, 1981), or Charles M. Fair's *The Dying Self* (Middletown, CT: Wesleyan University Press, 1969).
30. Rifkin, 208.
31. Rifkin, 6–7.
32. Rifkin, 7.
33. Rifkin, 3.
34. Rifkin, 206–7.
35. Rifkin, 238–40.

5

FAILURE IN TIME

When a person experiences or is asked to experience an event as a failure, a particular kind of interpretation is advanced about the event and the person's relationship to that event. The significance of any failure is measured relative to an individual's identity and a situation in which that individual is in some way involved or is at risk. A failure is only significant for individuals if it intrudes upon a context of events and relations that is significant for the individual. A part of this context is an individual's perception of time and continuity.

The attribution of failure interrupts some sequence of events and relationships that otherwise would be perceived as continuous and ongoing. Interpreting something as failure takes attention away from the continuity and focuses it on a moment in time. There is a time-line of contextual events, including patterns of experiences and expectations, that manifests the evidences and consequences of failure. Consider a very ordinary occurrence. A shoelace comes untied. This might occur while one is dressing. In that case, the sequence interrupted easily allows for retying the shoe. The incident is negligible; the fault is rectified without embarrassment or perhaps even without real notice. Should the shoe come untied in public, whether when walking on the street with a friend or approaching the platform to receive an award, the same event interrupts a significant sequence of social events. One can imagine situations in which personal variables could make this event especially embarrassing: for a small child wishing to prove his or her skill, for a handicapped person, or for a politician working a crowd. It is possible even with such a trivial incident that "fault" will be assigned and that character attributions will be made.

Insofar as an event is perceived as a failure, even this mundane instance shows that: (1) A sequence of events is interrupted by awareness that something has gone wrong. Perception of fault discontinues a sequence of action that the individual had hoped would succeed. (2) The competence, intentions, or capacities of any person at fault come into

85

question. Failure occurs. To establish what kind of failure and what degree of failure has occurred, the failure must be located in a context of actions that includes both past history and future expectations or goals.

In this chapter I turn to the uses of themes associated with past and future. Past and future are inescapable topics in discourse that deals with failure. When failure interrupts a sequence, one must find either an interpretation that reestablishes continuity between past and future, or discover some program of change that involves a productive pattern of making past and future discontinuous. Very often both interpretive moves are implicit. That is, change itself can be interpreted as a way of producing a new continuity between past as understood and future as expected or desired. The general problem–solution structure of dealing with failure uses "past" to identify and analyze the problem and "future" to propose a solution and picture the consequences of solutions.

The functions associated with the past–future *topos* were dramatically apparent in the examples discussed in the preceding chapter. Evidences of present failure were located and defined with reference to past and future in order to create understanding of and evaluate the significance of the failure. Past causes and future consequences were offered to shape and motivate resolutions to failure. Ehrlich's use of past–future framing was especially complex: a hypothetical future was described from a future "present," one that looked back at the past, which was really the audience's present. Ehrlich used population trends as the scientific basis for his certainty about this future, abstracting from the past and assuming continuity in the future. Toffler began with a historical analysis of change, using the past to establish the continuity of change. He then cited evidences of present change to project that continuity into the future. Skinner gave very brief treatments of historical causes and present failures, and the determinism of his treatments was crucial to his overall argument. Whereas Skinner seemed to be gripped by a utopian future, we were led to consider what of the past would be recovered in this future. Rifkin used the inevitable future as the context for evaluating present actions and choices, and he sought to actualize a distant past ideal in his proposed new covenant. The apocalyptic presentations of these authors made their past–future themes extreme, but the themes identify the general functions of the past–future *topos* in therapeutic rhetoric. The definitions of the failure, the evaluations of the failure's significance, the individual's responsibility for the failure, and the possibilities and requirements for solution of the failure were all developed using themes calling up the past and future.

Discussions of past causes and of future consequences are two of the more obvious uses of past–future relationships. An interpretation of a cause–effect sequence positions a failure in a context where its significance can be evaluated and some solution can be proposed. The nature of a failure in the present will inevitably shape the expected or desired future that is constructed. What is less obvious is that ideas about the past need to be shaped and reshaped in order to understand and treat failures as they occur in the present, and this is one important function of the past–future *topos* I wish to explore in this chapter.

In therapeutic rhetoric the uses of past–future themes are tied directly to the persuasive designs of the rhetoric. Consolatory persuasion attempts to get persons to accept failure as a natural outgrowth of events. The failure is often treated as inevitable, absolving the individual of responsibility. In such persuasion, the past provides a context in which to diminish or explain present failure. Compensatory persuasion, on the other hand, seeks to promote some kind of change. The future must therefore be treated as the context for interpreting present or past failures. One aims to erase past failure or meliorate its effects, reducing the failure to its reparable components. Complete therapeutic persuasion seeks to separate the individual from a failure sequence through new understanding of what that sequence is, promote some change of self within the boundaries of possible repair, and reestablish continuity of self within some new, better perspective on the failed sequence. The ability of individuals to perform this therapeutic process rhetorically requires manipulation of past–future relationships.

Another way of viewing past–future operations in the therapeutic process is to observe when change is warranted and when permanence is established. Failure is announced, experienced, or defined as a disruption between past and future. Failure breaks a continuity between an understanding of the past and an expected future. When that failure is explained, the past must be reconstructed to show how it held the potential and the cause of the failure. If one is to be motivated to change this failure sequence, the future must be reconstructed in light of the failure. A new future must be constructed to hold potential remedy, or the future must be revalued so it can hold that potential. At this juncture, past and future, as redefined or revalued, are seen as a potential continuity. There must be some break in this failure sequence if repair is to be accomplished. Change is presented as a way of reestablishing continuity between past and future, as now understood. Some new, better, or more highly valued continuity is established between the now changed and formerly faulty agent and the new world and the past. In other words, the failed past must be redeemed, and this redemption is performed by constructing a new continuity, a continuity that transcends the failure sequence.

It is not my object to provide a taxonomy of all possible uses of the *topos* past–future. I simply want to emphasize that in therapeutic rhetoric we invest the past or future and their relationship with selected qualities that address failures and their solutions. There is much more rhetorical logic in our constructions of past and future than standard historical or scientific methods admit. The ways in which we assign qualities to temporal relationships can be seen in interpretations of history.

Two basic sorts of historical interpretation are therapeutically useful: (1) those that emphasize permanence or continuity in temporal development, and (2) those that emphasize principles of change. In the first kind of interpretation, superordinate principles or values are extracted from history and offered as a basis for transcending failure. Identification of self with such permanencies allows one to perceive continuity in spite of momentary failures. In the second kind of treatment, principles of change are offered as bases for transforming failures. Identification of self with larger forces of change gives one the necessary mechanisms, modes, or models for executing change in identity or actions. As I have noted, the two processes are often interwoven. One can see a transcendent unity between past and future as a basis for personal transformation to accord with this larger principle. Or, conversely, one may see a larger concept of change as itself a transcendent principle that provides continuity between past and future. Identification with this principle then yields the kind of transcendence of momentary failure that is sought.

These moves were illustrated in Toffler's use of change as an inevitable principle of development. Change, reified as an unavoidable part of self and society, became the basis both for compensations and for a transcendent principle that in a sense redeemed the disturbing experiences of change that the audience suffered in the present. This feature is also apparent in evolutionism and the Marxist view of history. There is in both views a continuous history of revolutions and changes. A theory of orderly progressions is posited. When consolation is sought, the Marxist or evolutionist can say that outcomes are preordained by the orderly past. When compensation is sought, either evolutionist or Marxist can pronounce that evolution or revolution is the larger pattern of change, and we must identify with and participate in that process.

Mircea Eliade has analyzed therapeutic uses of history in religious rituals. He believes that cultures hold two different senses of time, "sacred" time and "profane" time.[1] Sacred time is the mythic past. In many primitive and non-Christian cultures this past is symbolized as an "eternal present," where the linear sequence of past–present–future is absent. Through ritual, Eliade believes, participants bring this sacred time into their immediate presence; sacred meanings are renewed and revitalized, and members are then reoriented for "ordinary temporal duration" with their experience now invested with the sacred qualities of their mythic past. Rites, in Eliade's view, are symbolic patterns whereby individuals may "pass without danger from ordinary temporal duration to sacred time."[2]

To illustrate how similar rhetorical processes occur in contemporary Western society, I offer a particularly interesting scene from Thornton Wilder's fiction. In *The Eighth Day*, Wilder portrays the townsfolk of Coaltown, Illinois, gathered under the community clock at the town hall. It is just before midnight, New Year's Eve, 1899. The scene is an especially important observance of time's passing. The community awaits the new century, and the people turn to the town's most articulate citizen, Dr. Gillies. They ask Dr. Gillies, the man most familiar with the "new" science, what "the new century will be like." Gillies perceives the insecurity and apprehension of his audience, and he delivers a consoling speech in which he "lied for all he was worth." Gillies extemporized:

> Nature never sleeps. The process of life never stands still. The creation has not come to an end. The Bible says that God created man on the sixth day and rested, but each one of those days was many millions of years long. That day of rest must have been a short one. Man is not at an end but a beginning. We are the children of the Eighth Day.[3]

Wilder depicts the blend of religion and evolution that was common in the late nineteenth century, and though Gillies was "lying," the speech reflects his sense that some reconciliation between the two sets of beliefs is needed.

As the scene is played out, some of the audience recognize "godless evolution" in Gillies' construction of the past, and they leave the town hall. The doctor continues, describing the phases of evolution as understood by the science of the day. Wilder has him address the young boys in the group:

> Life! Why life! What for? To what end? Something came out of the ooze. Where was it going? [The boys murmur, "To man." Gillies continues.] . . . The new man is emerging. Nature never sleeps.

89

Hitherto the sporadic great man, the lone genius, has carried the children of fear and inertia on his coattails. Henceforth, the whole mass will emerge from the cavedwelling condition . . . where most men cower still—terrified of encroachment, hugging their possessions, in bondage to fears of the thunder god, fears of the vengeful dead, fears of the untamable beast in themselves.

Mind and spirit will be the next climate of the human. The race is undergoing its education. What is education? [referring to the boys] . . . It is the bridge man crosses from the self-enclosed, self-favoring life into a consciousness of the entire community of mankind.

We learn that Gillies is himself pessimistic, that he had "no doubt that the coming century would be too direful to contemplate," but that he lied about the future for the sake of the boys. Gillies lied because "it is the duty of old men to lie to the young. Let those encounter their own disillusions. We strengthen our soul, when young, on hope; the strength we acquire enables us later to endure despair as a Roman should."

In this scene, past and future are invested with interpreted meanings. The context in which Wilder's citizens enact this rite is a therapeutic one. Wilder lets us know that the failures and problems they experience day to day have everything to do with the enormous changes that were then occurring in society and beliefs. New Year's Eve is the ritualized occasion for contemplating what change will bring. Through Gillies, Wilder symbolizes the meaning of this event marked by the threat of change. Gillies provides a theory of change that affirms historical stability and thereby implies a hopeful future. Failure is defined as the parochialism and materialism of the past, and a consoling future is found in a collective spiritual renewal. The principle of change is invested with spiritual values, and the progression from the past to the future is established as a continuity that erases the failures of the past and lessens those of the present. By these means, the audience is allowed to participate in a kind of time that is eternal, where past and future are integrated and consistent.

Gillies' speech points up the therapeutic function of beliefs about the past and their relationship to present failures and future life. The scientific interpretation is made to substitute for the religious.

Gillies reconciled the two accounts by stretching out the "days" of creation. He could thereby incorporate the notion of evolutionary progress within the audience's frame of past. The boys, at least, could see that evolution culminates in human development—in a future of achievement rather than of loss and conflict. Gillies showed his audience a legitimate way of passing from a too parochial past to a future where progress could remedy the world's ills.

Wilder pictures his Coaltowners as fearful of change. The growth of science, materialism, and mass society seemed to them a threat to continuity between a familiar past and an intelligibile future. But Wilder put in Gillies' mouth rhetoric that consolingly portrayed the past as *both* sacred and progressive. The material and scientific changes no longer constituted a break in a secure past. Incipient change was now portrayed as a perfecting outgrowth of the past as Gillies reinterpreted it. The past was made a failure sequence, and the new past–future continuity promised an orderly and ongoing repair of that failure.

A good deal of therapeutic rhetoric fuses sacred elements of the past with present and future themes in something like the way Eliade observed. This format is so common to political persuasion that it becomes a ceremony of sorts. Our historic traditions are recalled and their sacredness is fused with remedial beliefs and actions that are recommended. For example, the wisdom of the Founding Fathers in establishing a system of checks and balances can be extolled and applied to the future in celebrating Constitution Day, and it can as readily be extolled and applied in arguing for or against corrective laws, regulations, or compromises between the executive and legislative branches of government. In short, our sanctified traditions are repeatedly called up to explain problems, and the future is then constructed accordingly. When this is done, the audience participates in the social order in a way sanctified through ritualistic persuasion.

The notion that we can and do spiritualize time throws new light on the rhetoric of the authors discussed in chapter 4. Those men presupposed a kind of continuity-granting sacredness for evolution and for social change. Carrying forward such a sanctified principle found in the past enabled the scientifically oriented apocalyptics to construct a future that is a spiritual, collective, and even eternal time where there are no qualifications and penalties. Such a vision can provide consolation for present and past failures, and motivation for compensatory actions in the present.

Any person's location in the world has reference to time. When failure is perceived, time frames can be seen as loci of the failure and perhaps its cause, or they can be seen as loci of opportunities for repair. Whichever is the case, past–future will become an indispensable *topos* for the rhetoric made about failure. When we look at therapeutic uses of this *topos,* we discover that past and future are not simply two stages of temporal relationship; they are also "places" where a person's identity can be rhetorically situated for therapeutic analysis and change. Selves of past time can be perfected in present and future time. Selves of the future can be protected by reforming selves in the present to correct faults of the past. In short, when therapeutic change is proposed, one simply cannot avoid making arguments about identities "placed" in the past, the present, and the future. Phenomenological inquiry into the ways that meaning is constructed in temporal frameworks helps to develop our understanding of the past–future *topos* in therapeutic rhetoric.

BECAUSE-OF AND IN-ORDER-TO CONTEXTS

Modern phenomenologists consistently identify the temporal nature of experience as the most important element in structuring and understanding experience. With little variation, phenomenological analysis posits that there is a profound difference between the structure of experience that occurs to us in ordinary temporal duration (Eliade's "profane" time) and the reflexive, cognitive apprehension of temporal experience. Many analysts refer this distinction to one that Bergson made between "living within the stream of experience and living within the world of space and time." The distinction also parallels William James's distinction between "knowing of" and "knowing about."

A particularly fruitful analysis of these two modes of temporal perception is found in the work of Alfred Schutz. Schutz formulated the experiences of "spatiotemporal time" and "ordinary duration" as two different "meaning contexts" for the interpretation of "meaningful lived experience."[4] He designated these two contexts as the "because-of" and the "in-order-to." Within these two contexts the individual is so situated in relationship to experience that two different kinds of "motives" can be interpreted. Schutz demonstrates that the because-of motives are constructed by reference to the past and that the in-order-to motives are constructed by reference to the future. He posited that "the structure of our experience will vary according to whether we surrender ourselves to the flow of duration or stop to reflect upon it, trying to classify it in temporal modes."[5] In the former experience one is "immersed" in a "stream" of fluctuating experiences to which one "surrenders." Reflection stops the progress of this flow in order to apprehend it with spatiotemporal concepts or structures. In this case, one steps completely out of the stream of experience in order to see one's reflection in that stream. By Schutz's reasoning, a person cannot reflect or consciously abstract from experience while immersed in duration. Every conscious examination of

92

temporal experience "stops" duration and employs interpretative "schemes" to reflect on the meaning of experience.

If we agree with Schutz and other phenomenologists that there are two modes of temporal experience, we imply that there are two modes of interpreting any experience. More importantly for rhetorical theory, if we think or talk about being in duration, we inevitably step outside of duration and interpret it with what Schutz calls spatiotemporal concepts and what others call symbols.

How we experience the two kinds of time is easily illustrated if we think of moving pictures. There we can have a sense of time that operates like the movie projector; we experience a continuous succession of moments in which actions and events emerge and are experienced in the ordinary duration of the movie. However, when we have experienced an episode, we can turn back upon the whole of the experience, describe its developments from beginning to middle and end. Often we see how early events of the film foreshadowed or caused events that we learned only later in the movie. This is in principle the difference between in-order-to and because-of analysis.

Schutz perhaps does not do enough to demonstrate that the interpretive structures one develops through reflective experience actively influence one's interpretations while experiencing duration. Past experiences create interpretive frames and expectations that influence how we experience events in sequence, and what the sequences themselves are. Likewise, the structures that are useful for interpreting duration will also influence the structuring of reflective analysis. For instance, we may only experience things in sequence and fail to reflect on any other meaning or motive. The important point is that both in-order-to and because-of contexts are interpretive frameworks available at any given time; they both employ symbolic or spatiotemporal structures, and they yield quite different orientations toward the meanings of actions and events.

The in-order-to and because-of distinction helps to identify the interpretive potentials of the past–future *topos*. In-order-to motives are those that are directed at some desired or expected future. An individual sees actions as having meaning in their successive progress toward an outcome. Because-of motives are possible only when one looks back at the past. We can interpret past actions and events with knowledge of their outcomes, and therefore claim they happened "because."

Failure is an event in time. Normally it occurs while we are pursuing some goal. The failure has meaning within the context of that goal and the sequence of actions undertaken to achieve it. This is the in-order-to context. If new actions or methods of achieving that future goal can be prescribed, one compensates; new in-order-to motives are generated. But failure also can cause us to stop our pursuit of the goal, to look back on the experience and assess the meaning of the failure. If failure obliterates the success of the sequence, one needs to be consoled. This involves turning toward the because-of context of interpretation and the kind of motives that are attributed therein.

In the because-of context, actions and events are sequenced with reference to a past point of origin. The meaning of one's actions is no longer ordered by an expected outcome. The present is seen as the outcome of some past event or development. In this context one can see that present circumstances happened because of antecedents and causes. The interpretation of sequences in this context will take form as an account of how the present came to be.

One can readily see how interpretations of failure figure into this motivational vocabulary. I am writing this book. That action can be interpreted with reference to some future goal. Motives of success could easily figure: earning tenure, establishing a career, seeking admiration or promotion, etc. "Just getting it off one's chest" might be a suitable interpretation, where achieving completion would itself be the success of a sequence of actions. Time is treated as flowing forward in this case, and any failures that are suffered have meaning within that forward motion of personal and identity-related sequences. Because-of interpretations are also possible. One might say that writing a book reveals motives of overachievement, compulsion, failure in other occupations, unhappy childhood, social alienation, ego-maniacism, ad absurdum. The therapeutic vocabularies of psychological diagnostics readily reveal the because-of context; current conditions are explained as outcomes of past episodes or events. Notice too that these are all identity-related causes. Identity is itself understood in both because-of and in-order-to contexts. Failure generally requires that we turn to the because-of context to assess and give explanations of the failure, but we also return to the in-order-to context to compose compensations and redirect future goals.

Schutz observed that when one uses the because-of context to construct the meaning of lived experience, one chooses between past actions that seem to have been motivating and those that were not.[6] At a given moment in the in-order-to sequence, the ordering goal may be an ultimate goal or some intermediate goal that is needed in order to complete successive actions. A given failure may have reference to either kind of goal. The goal specifies the kind and degree of failure and the possibilities for successful compensation. In the because-of context, some past moment or action is selected as the beginning of a failed sequence. There are thus different bases for imposing order on the two sequences of the specified events. The two kinds of interpretations yielded are quite different, although in either stance taken toward a failure one is giving order to life experiences.

The difference between the two kinds of interpretive potentials can be illustrated with the familiar Christmas story of Scrooge. While Scrooge was acting in order to make more money, he possessed one set of values (individual and material). When he was enabled to see past–present–future as a whole, however, he discovered a different interpretation of his actions, yielding a completely new moral stance. Scrooge's because-of perspective allowed him to select meaningful events differently, see the consequences of his actions for self and others, embrace a new theory of life, and perceive different values (social and spiritual).

These features of the in-order-to and because-of stances have importance for rhetorical presentations concerning failure and its solutions. First, viewing phenomena from one position or the other circumscribes a person's options for understanding and responding to failure. Second, the principle of selectivity whereby failure is located in either a future or a past moment circumscribes the kinds and degrees of failure that are perceivable. If failure is pictured as blotting out an entire future goal or, as in the case of apocalyptic authors, an entire future, then the avenues to either consolation or compensation are limited. The selection of some past moment and the construction of a meaningful sequence involving failure that derives from an originating failure is especially important. Whether this time is rooted deeply in the human past, as in Gillies' speech, or with an individual's childhood, or in training for a career, or only at the point where one formulated a plan makes an enormous amount of difference to the qualitative way the failure is experienced. Furthermore, therapeutic theories all utilize interpretations that point to significant events of the past which preordained the kind and degree of failure that present troubles represent. Psychoanalysis, behaviorism, existential therapy, and virtually all therapeutic schemes posit because-of theories that are ready-made explanations for present failings. This is also true of religion and many uses of history and science: they support theories which create sequences of past events, and when used to explain instances of failure they point to which events are most likely to be causal and motivational.

A further implication of Schutz's analysis is that because-of theories become frameworks for interpreting and acting in the present. Failures occur in in-order-to orientations toward goals. When one fails, one typically must reflect backward to discover the origin and cause of the failure. One must then shift to the because-of orientation. This is where theory about past causes and motivations may guide interpretations that formulate the failure in greater generality than would be warranted by the specific case alone. We know, for instance, that some religious persons take momentary failures as signs of sin, evil, or other larger causal forces that their because-of theories specify. Those immersed in psychiatric theory will see failures as indications of problems that they have corroborated with their therapists. This is a general feature of interpretation that Burke has described: "Piety" for our senses of "what goes with what" leads us to base our expectations for the future upon formulated descriptions of motive. Symbolic orientations can thus function as "psychoses" that prescribe our interests and interpretations.[7] Once understanding is constructed in a because-of sequence, it is necessary that a new in-order-to sequence be constructed that turns toward the future with either reformed goals or reformed means to achieve the original goals. In sum, the way that failure is interpreted within sequences of past developments and future outcomes will circumscribe an episode of meaningful lived experience that is damaged or destroyed by failure.

This analysis adds two important points to Schutz's discussion of in-order-to and because-of contexts. First, these constructions of past and future orientations are symbolic. It is by using symbols drawn from conceptions of the past or the future that constructed sequences and interpretations can manipulate understanding of human experience and provide rationales for action. Second, the operations and symbolic manipulations of these meaning contexts are interactive. It is impossible that either meaning context should be used exclusively to manage any particular episode of human experience. In-order-to goals are formulated through reflection in because-of contexts. Sequences of action are constructed according to interpretations of what has and has not worked in the past. Similarly, because-of explanations arise at least in part from previous sequences of in-order-to actions. In the case of ritual behaviors such as those Eliade discusses, in-order-to sequences of past orientations may be incorporated as part of the symbolic meaning of the past, and may greatly influence our explanatory theories and hence our selection of meaningful, causal events of the past.

Construction of meaningful lived experience requires choosing among rhetorical treatments of past and future, and therapeutic treatment of failure requires that those rhetorical treatments construct understanding of experience and frameworks for repair. The rhetoric must also do this in ways that make the past and future consistent. Goals and action sequences must be constructed in light of past failures; past and present failures must be understood in terms of goals and purposeful actions that were once part of a future-oriented attempt at success. With these additions to Schutz's analysis of temporal consciousness, we may consider the kinds of functions that are performed by recourse to themes of past–future analysis when failure is being addressed.

TRANSFORMATION AND TRANSCENDENCE

The classical example of Oedipus provides a good starting point for considering the roles of superordinate theories in examining the past and projecting the future. Oedipus' tragic career was "fated." But fate is itself a theory that posits a continuity and interaction between past and future. It also integrates themes of self–society and spiritual–material. Fate is a because-of construction. When one looks back at the past as fated, one can see how actions were determined. Yet this because-of theory of fate also explains the truth of a prophecy about the future. Oedipus acted in order to avoid his fate. While on the road to Delphi, in an in-order-to succession of actions, he meets and kills Laius, who interferes with Oedipus' goals. In the in-order-to context, Oedipus was being kingly and displaying courage. When he learns that he killed his father and that his "kingly" actions were failures, Oedipus must turn to the theory of fate to understand and assess his failure. At this point he might have been consoled that he could not have acted otherwise, but instead he feels that some response must be made and some balance be created. He compensates with self-mutilation (mortification). Without his understanding and evaluation of his failure, interpreted with the theory of "fatedness by the gods," his response of self-mutilation would have no meaning. In the interpretive context of the situation, Oedipus' failure was not that he mistakenly killed his father, but that he failed to avoid his prophesied fate. His failure was interpreted as a matter of personal identity, *hubris,* and it thus demanded that he personally suffer. By taking his failure personally and responding to it personally, Oedipus kept his personal importance intact. That is, he could still see himself as personally selected for the wrath of the gods. His extreme response was then not only a fitting penance for his *hubris,* it also reaffirmed his importance in the total scheme of things. From this point of view, we can say that Oedipus' failure was that of not integrating the because-of theory of fatedness with his in-order-to scheme.

The tale of Oedipus also helpfully illustrates the two primary ways of resolving failures. One can transform oneself in order to integrate the self with the flow of events in time, and/or one can transcend an immediate

97

failure by identifying with some overarching, enduring principle governing past–future relations. "Fatedness" could have provided Oedipus with grounds for transcending his failure, as it did for his tragic counterpart Sisyphus. Oedipus could have seen himself as part of a narrative unity running inevitably from past to future. This would place the meaning of Oedipus' life and deeds above isolated actions and provide consolation for his error. But Oedipus had invested his identity and life in an inorder-to sequence, and he did so to cheat the prophesy. After he made that mistake, his transformation was called for, a transformation he executed dramatically in self-humiliation. His transformation reestablished the consistency of his actions with fatedness. Moreover, having transformed himself, Oedipus could now find grounds for transcendence. He was now reconnected with the transcendental laws of fatedness. Thus, transcendence and transformation are not mutually exclusive. As with Scrooge, finding ways of transcending linear time can reveal "true" order and values that show one how to transform self.

The functions of transformation and transcendence also call for use of the other *topoi* of therapy. Self and social relationships are involved, as are spiritual and material orientations. My principal concern here is to show what must happen with past–future interpretations and relationships for transformative and transcendent functions to occur. In the process I have isolated the special role of the past–future *topos* in achieving consolation and compensation. There must be some dialectical manipulation of because-of and in-order-to meanings to achieve transformation and transcendence. Transformation is largely an in-order-to activity, yet it requires because-of analysis. Transcendence requires largely a becauseof orientation, relying on nontemporal guidance for interpreting the past, yet it requires a certain degree of in-order-to analysis.

The use of because-of analysis to create schemes of transformation is generously illustrated in contemporary therapeutic rhetoric that calls for personal transformation. The contemporary savant Werner Erhard has founded an extensive network of therapy seminars called *est*, of which there have been several popular imitators. The doctrine and techniques of *est* are not published, but they are available to those who pay the expensive training costs and attend the seminars. Erhard has, however, collaborated on his biography, which portrays his life story, conversion, and formulation of the *est* doctrine.[8] It appears that identity transformation has been a lifelong strategy in Erhard's dealings with failure. He changed his name from Jack Rosenberg to Jack Frost when he began selling automobiles and to Werner Erhard when he began selling identity transformation. The biography offers an analysis of Erhard's childhood and changes, recalling the fervent conversion of his father from Judaism to Christianity. This conversion appears to have been strategically important to Erhard, because the logic of his doctrine of personal transformation is very near to that of Christian conversion. The biography mentions the incident, then quickly notes how much Werner took after his father. One is given the sense that Werner's quest and commitment are as much spiritual as those of any religious seeker.

The autobiographical approach of the book gives Erhard opportunity to legitimize his personal credibility and his methods of converting others. The work spells out the theoretical rationale that Erhard devised while managing the events of his life, and it depicts the many stages of development in his understanding of life. All of these new understandings of life seem to come after one kind of failure or another. By the time he developed *est,* Erhard's quest had led him to synthesize every therapeutic and success theory from Freud through Dale Carnegie to Scientology. Erhard's life story explains and validates a vocabulary of motives used in his theory and techniques. While he is cautious not to reveal any of the in-order-to motives that his seminars sell, Erhard's biography gives a persuasive account of the because-of rationale that legitimizes his training and advice. In Erhard's construction of this rationale for transformation, we have an opportunity to observe how because-of and in-order-to contexts are made consistent with each other, and how the past is composed in a fashion that legitimizes a particular kind of solution.

The very first lines of Erhard's biography say: "This is a story about true and false identity, and about who each of us really is. It is couched in the form of the life history of someone named Werner Erhard, an imposter by destiny and by choice, who went on a fateful journey of self-discovery." The meaning of Erhard's life is made to seem no less profound than that of Oedipus, and this view of the past leads us to expect the events to foretell "destiny" and "fate," and therefore to possess deep symbolic significance. The readers are invited to join in a reflective search for true identity, to inspect their own pasts through identification with Erhard, and together forge the justifications for self-change. That the review of Erhard's past is intended to convince everyone that their present identities are failures is clear: "The first thing to learn on the road to one's true self is that one is not who one thinks one is. Each person, without exception, has a fictitious past; each of us, is, precisely, an imposter."[9] Armed with a theory very much like Oedipus' fatedness, we are to set out on a quest that will yield true selfhood and, by eliminat-

99

ing or debunking elements of our pasts, make our personal transformations possible.

According to Erhard, our normal understandings of our pasts are invalid. Our because-of motives suffer from lack of clarity and understanding. The past is mysterious, and we must use Erhard's theory to examine his past in order to discover the real motives that lurk there and in our own pasts. Not only is Erhard's theory being legitimized in this autobiographical exercise, but his current identity as a powerful savant is revealed as predestined by the meanings of childhood events. The book tells us that when one searches for "true identity, one steps in a labyrinth, a maze, a tunnel of love, a hall of mirrors, a derelict graveyard, a long-neglected archeological site."[10] Erhard has made it through this labyrinth, but without the leader and his theory, readers will remain forever lost in their searches for true identity.

Werner's accidents as a young boy provide data that call for because-of examination. Unconscious and failure-laden motives are attributed to the poor five-year-old who falls a lot and who is hurt in a car wreck. The biographer explains that "an accident can serve, unconsciously, to attract attention to oneself; it can also act as a form of self-punishment. It is a common unconscious mechanism for dealing with feelings of guilt and with the experienced threat of punishment."[11] This exercise in psychiatric logic endows Erhard's early life with deep meaning. It attributes because-of motives even to a car wreck where the five-year-old could not have been the driver. Everyone reading the book is invited to examine his or her own childhood accidents for evidence of such guilt and expiation, to find the narrative grounds for his or her own history of mysterious failures and unconscious motivations. The reader is made to feel a need for some system of uncovering and organizing data about his or her past. It is pointed out that Erhard's theory is not that of Freud, but Freudian explanation is used to legitimize the basic task of because-of examination by linking it with some therapeutic theory: "Whatever the real explanation may be" for the boy's mishaps, "little Jack Rosenberg was quite unconscious of all these things, and it would be up to Werner Erhard, many years later, to discover the patterns in his past, and to complete his relationship with it. When he did so, he would choose patterns of analysis and explanation that differed from Freud's."[12] The entire childhood is imbued with failure: unconscious motives of guilt, failure to understand, failure to use the accident for some self-constructive purpose.

The narrator examines Erhard's past in detail, but with great selectivity. A parade of theoretical insights is thus introjected into the narrative in Erhard's own voice. This is an interesting rhetorical technique, for while Erhard's biography is presented as impersonal and separated from him in the narration, the theoretical perspective that gives meaning to that past comes from the propounder of *est*, the now transformed Erhard. Erhard's voice-over of the theoretical, enduring meanings of events allows the biographer to switch time frames. The because-of theory comes in the savant's voice, from a future where all of these tensions have been resolved, but the narrator is in the past where these events unfold. He is applying Erhard's theory to the false in-order-to motives of the young Rosenberg. Rosenberg's experiences are common: youthful alienation, early marriage and children, new jobs, moving from place to place, love affairs, marital problems, and divorce. All are familiar experiences and problems for the age 25–40 audience that has embraced the *est* philosophy. The mundane sequences of their lives perhaps had great personal meaning; but until they came to this book, the events had no overarching theoretical significance such as Erhard is able to spin forth.

The biographical narrative gives those experiences special significance as pattern; they fit Erhard's because-of theory. In the narrative of Erhard's life, such experiences are shown to reveal a kind of flaw in his past identity(ies?) and self-knowledge, a flaw that resulted in the repetition of failed in-order-to pursuits and goals. Erhard's rather mundane past becomes a story of everyone's fate and destiny. Readers are led to the conclusion that their own pasts also have great meaning, that their past and present dissatisfactions and failures are embedded in a fictitious past, that they have constructed false identities from the materials of their pasts, and that they need a theory with which to organize and interpret the motives that have led them to their present senses of failure. Whatever the reader or potential *est* convert had previously sensed as failure or frustration has at this point been redefined: All failures past and present were due to inadequate knowledge about self and failure. This thematic focus creates an appetite for the particular kind of transformation that Erhard's training seminars sell.

The biography does not gives a straightforward rationale and description of the transformational scheme that Erhard advocates in his seminars. We do know, however, that his system depends on a special because-of interpretation of the past and a new in-order-to-design for the future. We also have the account of Erhard's own transformations, especially the one that brought him to be Werner Erhard, creator of *est*. So, how and for whom does the because-of exposition of the book provide therapy? Its rhetorical appeal to readers is a special blend of therapeutic theory and "success counseling."

It may be that the most common users of Erhard's biography are persons already initiated in the *est* cult. The book was not widely promoted, and a merely curious reader would have his or her curiosity sated by the book alone. But followers who have attended, say, a couple of weekend seminars will have "bought into" the idea of personal transformation and Erhard's particular in-order-to motivations. These readers would need to (1) complete their personal transformations by realigning their pasts under the auspices of the already accepted voice of Erhard, (2) replicate their experience of transformation at the seminar by vicariously participating in the leader's own story, and (3) internalize the principle of transformation as it is constructed in the because-of theory. Erhard's life story, his theory of transformation, and the reader's desire for renewal all suggest that one conversion or transformation is not enough, and that one must be able to repeat the process whenever one encounters failure in one's life.

The convert to *est* is most likely to come out of the seminar experience with a feeling of in-order-to alignment and purpose. When that alignment encounters resistance and problems, as inevitably it does, the individual must return to the because-of perspective to find the source of the problem and regain in-order-to success. Explanation of the failure and realignment of the in-order-to plan require reconstruction of the past according to the therapeutic principles on which *est* is grounded. Support for one's transformation can be had by collaborating with other *est* converts, which the book facilitates. Support can also be had by undergoing more lengthy and advanced *est* seminars, which the book seems to encourage. Such support can be further bolstered by greater identification with the leader and his own trials, and by greater theoretical involvement in the because-of theory he has created. In short, the elaboration of the because-of theory in the biography links up with the various in-order-to schemes and potential in-order-to failures that *est* followers are likely to experience. The book also helps to mend a flaw in the seminar style of conversion. Without the book converted persons would have no text to return to, no Bible to sustain and enhance their faith, and no rituals to perform beyond returning to the seminars. The only readers of the book I have encountered were full-fledged converts to the in-order-to orientation of *est*. They had completed the seminars and now they needed portable support and rituals for daily reinforcement of the beliefs of the system. Erhard's biography can fill these needs for them.

Burke's notion that "inspirational" literature performs therapy in the mere reading of the book seems relevant to Erhard's biography. The book could constitute a renewing ritual of transformation in compressed form. In this respect, however, Erhard's book differs from the plethora of self-help books in bookstores today. It does not spell out the in-order-to details of completing personal transformation. In popular existential therapies available in book form, the therapeutic process is intended to take place through reading and applying the book's counsel. Most of these books provide because-of rationales, the therapeutic theories of the authors, in condensed form. The books then go on to provide inspiration for undertaking in-order-to programs of self-change. The bridge between because-of theory and in-order-to actions is more crucial to the intentions of these books, and they illustrate the future element of the *topos* more completely than does Erhard's biography.

The paperback therapies begin with a truncated exposition of a because-of theory that its author has composed, one the reader is supposed to identify with and use to analyze his or her feelings of failure. Common feelings and senses of failure are described, and the therapists cite cases they have treated successfully. The therapist analyzes the basic problem in general terms that readers can apply to their own failures. The therapies offer some general or universal principle that causes individual failure. With this done, the past is quickly abandoned and a future-oriented perspective is adopted, showing how to transform oneself by changing the way one acts towards situations. In these treatments the because-of theory is explained in order to legitimize the solutions presented and to invite the reader's participation in the transformation scheme. To the extent that any transformation is realized through reading such a book, it is accomplished, as in Erhard's therapy, by debunking the past, creating new understanding of one's failures, and turning attention to one's future self and actions. Generally failure is announced as a discontinuity between past and future. Interestingly, this is commonly done by making one "aware of one's death." This is a strategy found in Christian revivals, existentialist perspectives, Erhard's book, and Scrooge's conversion. The strategy motivates belief in and desire for a new theory of because-of motives through which one can realign one's actions and make them consistent with desirable goals. Integration of identity with this new rendition of past-future consistency requires some transformation of the self. One should notice that this is precisely the same format used by the apocalyptic scientists discussed in chapter 4. The distinction between because-of and in-order-to rationales allows us to see the similarity of the patterns. The two rhetorical steps must at least implicitly establish the possibility that a reader could become consistent with the revelations of the agreed-upon because-of explanations of failure.

A doctrine of transformation is by definition an attempt to free oneself from a failed past by enabling a new self to integrate with reality through entering a new in-order-to sequence. Once transformed, however, a person will still confront further failures that will make it necessary for him or her to elaborate because-of contexts that allow interpretations of the failure. When one fails after reforming one's in-order-to actions, the in-order-to sequence used is invalidated, and one must explain the new failure. This is likely to require further elaboration of the because-of explanations formerly used—else one's transformation will also be invalidated. Transformative schemes, therefore, need to offer compensatory strategies to help the transformed realign themselves within the philosophy of the scheme as they carry out new in-order-to sequences. The compensatory possibilities must be kept consistent with the because-of explanations of the scheme, else the entire system of analysis breaks down. No "success scheme" is wise that closes off options for consolation, for some failure is inevitable.

A transformational scheme needs to provide resources for transcendence. This would be a main function of Erhard's biography for *est* converts. The book allows them to return to the because-of "roots" and consider these more deeply when setbacks are encountered. It reconnects them to the higher spiritual meanings and continuities of the system or faith. Scriptures and liturgies do the same for religious persons. All such materials offer symbolic constructions of past–future consistency with which persons can reidentify by enacting sequences of thought or action that are more meaningful or enduring that those damaged by past failures. Transcending in such cases involves trying to abandon the sequential, linear experience of time and find a "timeless" sense of being outside of linear time. In transcending one tries to position oneself beyond and above momentary failures experienced in linear time. Burke described this rhetorical accomplishment thus: "Moments separated in time are linked outside of time, their community being idealistically grounded in a transcendent self that is neither present nor past, but lies outside of both by reason of its ability to experience the present in terms of the past."[13]

In Erhard's transformative scheme a key concept is "personal space." One can in a sense return to that space when one's plans and goals fail and one seeks to renew one's transformation. From this space one looks back at the past and recollects the consistent threads of one's identity and progress, accounts for the failure, and then returns to a future orientation renewed with a larger sense of personal growth. In Augustine's confessions, just as in Erhard's, one finds the spatial metaphor of time thoroughgoing:

> All this I do within, in that huge court of my memory. . . . There also I meet with myself; I recall myself, what, where, or when I have done a thing; and how I was affected when I did it. . . . By these I do infer actions to come, events and hopes: and upon all these again do I meditate, as if they were now present.[14]

Some concept of being that transcends momentary or ordinary time seems therapeutically necessary. Even in the most transformative schemes one finds symbolic passage to a transcendent "place." We see this in Eliade's primitives, whose passage to the mythic past allowed them to transcend their momentary and mundane meanings, and also allowed them to return to their profane affairs recharged with the spiritual meanings of their past. We might say that Heidegger's famous *Being and Time* attempts to recapture some of this "primitive" attitude about time and meaning. Heidegger's focus on the "horizon" is spatial. Like Erhard's idea of personal space, it insists on futurity in orientations to world. Heidegger obviously sought to unify our orientations of past and future into one continuous sense of being-in-the-world. The present is ontologically flawed, tensed with dread, anxiety, and guilt; but the embrace of present provides the integration of the individual in time, focused on a horizon, actualizing the enduring meanings of the past in choices and actions toward the future. Thus Being is transcendent in Heidegger's scheme because it bridges the gap between past and future, although it is the transformative self that is the source of transcendence and unity between past and future.

Integration with linear time seems to be a therapeutic imperative in phenomenological views. Laing, for instance, concludes that "the loss of a section of the linear temporal series of moments through inattention to one's time-self may be catastrophic."[15] Hannah Arendt argues that modern thinkers believe this because they have lost "tradition."[16] Being is not discovered in some "place" like the Christian heaven or the sacred places of Eliade's primitives. For Kafka, Kierkegaard, Sartre, and others, Being is found in *self*.[17] As in Erhard's theory, this self is never really allowed to step out of the flow of successive time, but the self is itself the locus of transcendence. Continuities of past and future are somewhat discovered in and through individual experiences. What Arendt meant about existentialist thinkers was that for them there is no stable, traditional orientation to a past "which selects and names, which hands down and preserves, which indicates where the treasures are and what their worth is." For them "there seems to be no willed continuity in time and hence, humanly speaking, neither past nor future, only sempiternal change of the world and the biological cycle of creatures living within it."[18] In other words, such thinkers must find the basis for transcendence within sequential experience of time. The past confers no special sanctity or superordinate definition on kinds of experiencing. Hence moderns tend, as Arendt observes, to characterize the "space" that the individual occupies as the "place" where transcendent experiences must occur. This is why contemporary therapeutic rhetoric focuses on individual identity and argues that through understanding and transforming the self, success is achieved. This feature of therapeutic thinking helps to explain why there are so many acceptable because-of theories, and why individuals may embrace any and all therapeutic rationales that come along. The real need is for reintegration of in-order-to orientations and for doctrines that justify transformation to keep up with the flow of linear time. Perhaps this explains why therapies such as Erhard's are seldom undertaken with scrutiny, held to for very long, or applied with any real consistency. They are accepted as "any port in a storm" when a keen need for personal transformation is felt.

Relationship to time is an inescapable dimension of anyone's judgment of "success" or "failure." There seem, however, to be two kinds of time that can be used in weighing experience. One is time experienced as ordinary flow of successive events, and the other is what Eliade called sacred time or what Arendt saw as tradition—providing a sense of being that selects, names, preserves, and values that which stands beyond or above the experienced linear flow of time. The second kind of time allows discovery and identification of self with forces outside or beyond the self as it exists in ordinary time. Either past or future can be viewed as this second kind of time, as places where continuity can be found. Yet the first kind of time proceeds toward such a future, while the second proceeds from the past and to the present. The two ways of organizing experience are basic to therapeutic rhetoric and are reflected in the themes that I have epitomized as the past–future *topos*.

The contemporary cases I have cited indicate that most current therapies view problems as occurring within linear time and solutions as carried out in linear time. These therapies locate the place of problem resolution in the individual. One does not resolve problems by identifying transcendentally with forces or entities beyond the flow of ordinary experience of time. This means that transformation of selves rather than transcendence will be the solution most prominently proffered by the therapies. That is so, at least in theory. Upon closer examination, however, we see that transcendence is also a vital part of the way that these therapies use transformative rationales to bridge or repair disruptions in an individual's sense of integration with time. How much actual transformation takes place is and should be suspect. In evaluating self-help books and repeating self-help seminars, we should critically suspect that part of what is going on is the creation of a rhetoric that makes identity or self a kind of modern sacred ground. That is, these therapies are contemporary rituals by which a mythified, personal past is given sacred treatment and revisited in order to recharge the individual's participation in normal time with new meaning and energy. Although individuals participating in these rites attain symbolic transformation, there is a transcendent effect gained from the tranformative experience. It is difficult to say that any actual transformation is possible in the experience of rituals or therapies, hence it may be that symbolic transformation is but one way of transcending failure. From identifying with transformation, a basis for transcendence is also had. This is what Gillies tried to give the youths and what gives disciples of *est* their sense of "otherness." Recognition of change as the principle of existence gives Toffler's readers a kind of command over time that allows transcendence. So does recognition of one's place in nature's order for those counseled by Skinner and Rifkin's theories.

The predominant move in the rhetoric of contemporary therapies is to persuade people to make compensatory changes in themselves and their orientations toward the world. An in-order-to perspective and a focus on transformation provide the logic of this therapeutic advice. However, where rhetorical emphasis is on compensation, an effect may be to provide consolation. That is, rhetoric that offers a compensatory scheme for dealing with problems of failure may provide avenues to consoling transcendence by the very fact of promising compensation. The comprehensiveness of the therapeutic analysis can be consoling, and the simple ability to address human problems with rhetoric can in itself be partially consoling.

I believe I have shown that rhetoric aiming at transformation will use past–future themes in ways different from the ways those themes are used in rhetoric encouraging transcendence. Transcendence requires grounds other than integration with linear time; transformation, as contemporary therapies illustrate, may aim entirely at reintegrating the self with in-order-to realities. However, I hope to have shown that any transformative scheme will require separation from a perceived in-order-to sequence to theorize and reevaluate, employing transcendent moves. An implicit goal of any transcendent scheme is to enable persons to return to in-order-to functioning with renewed meanings, thus providing the basis for transformation.

This last consideration is crucial as I turn now to spiritual–material themes. The function of these themes is to aid in constructing spiritual–material relations in such ways that both transcendence and transformation are possible in coping with failure. Spiritual–material relations are treated as unities in which one may, in a sense, see timeless order and thus transcend momentary failures. They are also unities that provide transformative powers if they are understood and applied to remedy failures in the world.

NOTES

1. Mircea Eliade, *The Sacred and the Profane,* trans. Willard R. Trask (New York: Harcourt, Brace, 1959).

2. Eliade, 68.

3. Thornton Wilder, *The Eighth Day* (New York: Avon, 1976), 14–16.

4. Alfred Schutz, *The Phenomenology of the Social World,* trans. George Walsh and Frederick Lehnert (Evanston, IL: Northwestern University Press, 1967), 86–96.

5. Schutz, 45.

6. Schutz, 95.

7. Kenneth Burke, *Permanence and Change* (Berkeley: University of California Press, 1984), 37–49; 74.

8. William Warren Bartley III, *Werner Erhard: The Transformation of a Man, the Founding of est* (New York: C. N. Potter, 1978).

9. Bartley, 3.

10. Bartley, 9.

11. Bartley, 11.

12. Bartley, 13.

13. Kenneth Burke, *A Grammar of Motives* (Berkeley: University of California Press, 1969), 439.

14. *St. Augustine's Confessions,* trans. William Watts (London: William Heinemann, 1912), 97–98.

15. R. D. Laing, *The Divided Self* (New York: Random House, 1969), 116.

16. Hannah Arendt, *Between Past and Future* (New York: Viking, 1977), 3.

17. See Mark C. Taylor, *Kierkegaard's Pseudonymous Authorship: A Study of Time and the Self* (Princeton, New Jersey: Princeton University Press, 1975).

18. Arendt, 5.

6

THE PROCESSES OF SELF-UNIFICATION

The *topos* spiritual–material provides themes and characterizations involved in the healing processes of therapeutic rhetoric. Spiritual–material considerations are vital to effective recovery and reorientation when people suffer failure. In this chapter I will examine the special role and properties of this *topos*.

From the beginning of this book, I have noted the tendency for therapeutic rhetoric to generalize the conditions and meanings of particular failures and so arrive at abstract and universal grounds of treatment. This is an essential move in consoling, where seeing one's failure as related to a larger design serves to minimize one's responsibility for it. One can see the failure as a product of grander and more significant causes or forces. This kind of interpretation also can serve to aggrandize the individual, for now it is he or she who has been "selected" to be the object of significant forces in the world. This contributes to the processes of effective self-recovery, providing interpretive and evaluative grounds for self–unification.

This tendency to see failure in terms of universal conditions is most clear in dramatizations of failure common in religious sermonizing and in literature or drama. In those formats there is an explicit desire to depict universal and significant forces at work in individual cases. Often the depiction is of a conflict between good and evil, a prominent variant of spiritual–material interpretation. We also find explicit use of spiritual–material themes in philosophy, psychology, aesthetics, and political doctrines, where universal grounds of failure are very often formulated and defined in order to recommend universal principles or patterns of resolution. The ontologies of metaphysical systems—from Thales, Heraclitus, and Parmenides; to Kant, Hegel, Marx; and today in scientism, subjectivism, and the "new physics"—all rely upon formulations based on the spiritual–material *topos*.

Despite the universal character of spiritual–material formulations, we should not say that all instances of failure call for explicit treatment using spiritual–material themes. A basketball player who fails to score from the foul line would probably not invoke a doctrine of spiritual–material conflict in order to explain missing the goal. Even so, a player who consistently misses foul shots may begin to question qualities of his or her character, the virtues and pressures of competition, his or her commitment to the game, or physical constitution, or training, or talent. Spiritual–material analyses of these more general causes of failure are available, and often they are prominent. Again, the more that universal explanations for failure are sought, the more the interpretations will be treated by themes that can be subsumed under the *topos* spiritual–material. Those persons who operate intensively under spiritual–material theses will move readily from particular failings to universal analyses in terms of the spiritual–material. Thus, we might expect an intensely religious basketball player to see his or her failure as the product of pervasive earthly or spiritual fault, divine reward and punishment, or, in rare cases, demonic forces working in the world.

Recourse to spiritual–material themes is ubiquitous in rhetoric that addresses human problems of value. Very often rhetoric is avowedly informed by the assumption that there are two abstractable orders in the world and that these interact and can conflict with one another. Such a dichotomous analysis can be found in hundreds of formulations. We treat of God and man, of man and nature, of intellect and passion, of morality and instinct, of spirit and flesh, of the abstract and the concrete, of the ideational and the economic. The number of such dialectical pairs is enormous, and there are seemingly infinite variations and gradations of these divisions that can occur in interpretations of the conditions and structures of self and the world. Orders of spiritual and material existence or forces are posited, and values are accordingly assigned.

The relationships between the spiritual and material orders are usually conceptualized in one or another of these basic ways: the spiritual and the material can be seen as distinct and separate systems of order, giving rise to two different orientations and kinds of human values. They can be seen as coexisting and cooperatively interactive orders that are expressed in the needs, ambitions, accomplishments, or destiny of people. They can be seen as directly and absolutely conflicting with each other, making humankind and each individual battleground for control by one or the other. These relationships are available as explanations for what a given failure means, and they can be offered as premises for the resolution of failure. We may conceive that we have failed to balance spiritual and material considerations by giving each order its due. Then it may be said that our material pursuits have led to spiritual neglect, or that we must render unto Caesar that which is his. The proposition that these ubiquitous forces are needed to maintain the balance of the world can console us for failures and provide direction for compensations. Failures can be and often are explained as products of a division and conflict between spiritual and material forces. Resolutions will then entail sacrificing the material for the spiritual, or vice versa. We thus purify ourselves of the conflict. On the other hand, we may compose theories and actions which unite the spiritual and material symbolically. Where this is done, the meanings and properties of the spiritual or the material are infused with the properties of the other—as when loaves and fishes minister spiritually and materially at one and the same time, or as when Martin Luther King, Jr., brings the two realms together in dreamed-of resolution of social, historical, and spiritual failures.

The rhetorical usefulness and therapeutic effectiveness of spiritual-material ideas are not confined to any particular formulation of the dualism. Rather, the pragmatic basis for using the *topos* derives from the strategic advantages that can be gained by applying the *topos* in interpreting and managing experience. Whether one postulates a division, balance, or ultimate interfusion of the spiritual and material realms, one has appropriated a basis for explaining, ordering, valuing, and choosing meanings and actions within an ontological framework. This is to say that the spiritual–material *topos* is used to establish the grounds upon which one may claim to know the spiritual significance of phenomena and to give that claim evaluative meaning and rhetorical force.

Use of the spiritual–material *topos* is most apparent in general doctrines and formulations that (1) an individual formulates as resolutions and responses to consistent failures in life or failure in general, (2) an individual may appropriate from religion, aesthetics, philosophy, or general world views that are explicitly designed to compensate and console failure in general, or (3) an individual may invoke as a general principle or "theory" about failure when specific conditions or occurrences of failure arise. Again, spiritual–material themes are most useful in forging complete and comprehensive schemes for dealing with failure. Formulations of spiritual–material relations complete the healing and recovery processes by providing or bolstering (1) general orientations to and interpretations of the problem of failure, (2) security and knowledge that failures can be dealt with and success can be had, and (3) a language and a general set of consolatory and compensatory strategies that allow individuals to deal with their senses of failure—whether these failures be of self or society, of past or future, or of a spiritual or material nature. In

111

short, the spiritual–material *topos* is fundamental to rhetorical coping with failure, and themes drawn from this *topos* are apt to occur in any therapeutic rhetoric.

FUNCTIONS OF THE *TOPOS*

In chapter 2 I noted that a sense of failure often induces a condition that can be described as self-division. When people experience failure, they come to see their identities as somehow "halved" by the experience. This is particularly true where self–society conflicts arise. Conflicts that arise between self and society are internalized as a state of self-division. This is a common manifestation of guilt, where the assignment of fault and responsibility to the self results in a feeling of alienation from the world and motivates attempts at self-unification.

Seeing one's identity as divided can be considered a step toward resolution of failure. At this stage the individual has at least some analysis of fault and some theory that may lead to self-unification. Division, as in guilt, offers some intelligible relationship among the failed self, the cause of the failure, and relationships to a conflictive world. But the very sorting through of experience to attribute guilt implies that spiritual–material assignments have been made. Values imply spiritual–material distinctions, hence spiritual–material considerations are bound to be part of aligning oneself with self or society or past or future in order to resolve whatever conflicts one's failure has come to represent.

In brief, however we come to define, analyze, or interpret failure, composing therapeutic remedies requires finding some avenue of identification with the world. The division or fault that one experiences needs to be seen as a manifestation of a similar division or fault in the world. As Hoffer commented, "There is in us a tendency to locate the shaping forces of our existence outside ourselves. Success and failure are unavoidably related in our minds with the state of things around us."[1] Working to cure this problem in the world is often the vehicle for resolving the division in self. Is is possible to identify and undertake to solve self–society problems in the world (Skinner), or even past–future problems (Gillies or Toffler), but spiritual–material themes are also used in these cases because we seek identification with world. Our identity suffers the same divided state as does the world. This is a useful identification, for it holds out the promise that solutions can be found in the world, or that our problems can be solved by solving those found in the world.

112

The therapeutic elements and design of the recovery process are most clear where spiritual–material themes are used directly in analysis and interpretation of failure. Religious rhetoric, James observed, is set up to treat all instances of failure as products of spiritual–material conflict in order to recommend identification with the spiritual as the effective and self-unifying resolution. This process begins by subsuming all failures under one basic problem or sense of failure. Religious persons, James said, "sense that there is something wrong with us as we naturally stand," and conceive within that fault a solution wherein they "sense that we are saved from the wrongness by making proper connections." With these "simple, general terms" we can understand the psychology of religious experience. These terms, James continued,

> allow for the divided self and the struggles; they involve the change of personal centre and the surrender of the lower self; they express the appearance of exteriority of the helping power and yet account for our sense of union with it; and they fully justify our feelings of security and joy.[2]

Within this arrangement are the possibilities of transcendent relationships, where failed persons may sustain connections with a higher power. Or transformation is possible where personal change becomes the avenue to such connections.

What happens generally, James said, is that an individual "identifies his real being with the germinal higher part of himself," and he does so by becoming

> conscious that this higher part is coterminous and continuous with a MORE of the same quality, which is operative in the universe outside of him, and which he can keep in working touch with, and in a fashion get on board of and save himself when all his lower being has gone to pieces in the wreck.[3]

Defining one's fault in terms of spiritual–material, then, establishes that there are large, powerful forces in the world. This implies a fundamental or ontological failure in "natural" existence, but it also establishes the viability of enduring and spiritually correct alignment with the "better forces" in the world. Experiencing failure makes an individual substantially one with a flawed world, but it opens the possibility of oneness with a "MORE of the same quality."

James made it clear that he considered these therapeutic processes parts of a fundamental psychological pattern. He wrote that

> the process of remedying inner incompleteness and reducing inner discord is a general psychological process, which may take place with any sort of mental material, and need not necessarily assume the religious form. In judging the religious types of regeneration . . . it is important to recognize that they are only one species of a genus that contains other types as well.[4]

With the goal of understanding this general psychological pattern of recovery, James undertook to "sum up in the broadest possible way" the characteristics of religious life. According to James, these are the five general characteristics:

1. That the visible world is part of a more spiritual universe from which it draws its chief significance;
2. That union or harmonious relation with that higher universe is our true end;
3. That prayer or inner communion with the spirit thereof—be that spirit God or "law"—is a process wherein work is really done, and spiritual energy flows in and produces effects, psychological or material, within the phenomenal world.
4. A new zest which adds itself like a gift to life, and takes the form either of lyrical enchantment or of appeal to earnestness and heroism.
5. An assurance of safety and a temper of peace, and, in relation to others, a preponderance of loving affections.[5]

This, I repeat, seemed to James "one species of a genus that contains other types as well." The first three beliefs constitute justifications for rhetorical practices we can expect to observe wherever the spiritual is highly valued over the material. James's fourth and fifth characteristics are the rewards for achieving "union or harmonious relation" with the spiritual. This is a very important species of dealing rhetorically with failure.

As James theorized, these therapeutic functions of religious discourse can also be found in rhetorical formats not overtly religious. We found them in the address of Martin Luther King, Jr., Toffler's treatment of future shock, Skinner's willed participation in cultural evolution, and Gillies' speech promoting identification with the force of the new age. These discourses posited spiritual–material forces generally at work and at odds with each other, and they also sought to identify transcendent and transformative powers with which the individual could identify and with which some harmonious relation could be achieved.

James focused on doctrines and beliefs that elevate the spiritual and make the material its subordinate. this is almost universally the case in religious expression. But rhetoric can and often does elevate material considerations as superordinate to the spiritual. The same therapeutic value, and the same rhetorical motivation, can be found in materialist doctrines and beliefs: in the Marxist's fight for the cause, in the paradoxical motives of a Twain or Sartre to persuade us in a world they have determined is unchangeable, in the life force of G. B. Shaw, or in Skinner's cultural evolution. With the use of James's basic analysis, a more general description of the rhetorical functions of the spiritual–material *topos* can be formulated: (1) By using the spiritual–material division as a pattern for understanding the character of the world, an individual universalizes the world as two competing orders, and unifies those orders by aligning his or her actions and commitments with the superior element. (2) The spiritual–material analysis makes it possible to sort the data of experience evaluatively into good or bad, right or wrong, better or worse. This interpretive move gives meaning and continuity to experiences that are past, present, or anticipated. (3) The workings of order, conflict, and evaluation are construed in self-definition so that individual actions and worth are defined as manifestations of universal conflict or unifying interactions between the bifurcated orders.

Formulations of the relation between spiritual and material should be viewed as ways of managing human identity, as parts of the nature of being and acting in the world. People require both spiritual and material kinds of explanations if they are to give order and value to the features of any situation and to their places in that situation. There are three relationships between spiritual and material that can be posited; these constitute three general ways of understanding failure and composing resolutions through human action: (1) It may be contended that spiritual–material considerations were not appropriately balanced. (2) It may be argued that spiritual and material considerations have not been coordinated or ministered in successful ways. (3) It may be contended that a given failure, or failure generally, occurs only because people fail to appreciate some grander scheme of spiritual and material integration that the order of the world can reveal. No matter which response is made, individual identity participates intelligibly and meaningfully in the posited relationship of spiritual and material. Hence one's failures, conflicts, choices, and sufferings acquire meaning because they have their places in a universal pattern. Experience gains importance in a world that reaches beyond self, and experience acquires value through conformity or consistency with the spiritual and material orders. We can observe these functions in samples of rhetoric that employ the themes of spiritual–material analysis in various ways.

The three functional themes that James identified for spiritual–material analysis can readily be seen in the Christian Science doctrine, a clear instance of a "healing rhetoric." That doctrine, of course, denies the reality of the material and insists that the spiritual is the only reality. In her arguments for the superiority of the spiritual, Mary Baker Eddy sought to rehabilitate the normal ways of sorting spiritual and material phenomena. She wrote:

> In the material world, thought has brought to light with great rapidity many useful wonders. . . . Belief in a material basis, from which may be deduced all rationality, is slowly yielding to the idea of a metaphysical basis, looking away from matter to Mind as the cause of every effect. . . . Semi-metaphysical systems are one and all pantheistic, and savor of Pandemonium, *a house divided against itself.*
>
> From first to last the supposed coexistence of Mind and matter and the mingling of good and evil have resulted from the philosophy of the serpent. . . . The categories of metaphysics rest on one basis, the divine Mind. Metaphysics resolves things into thoughts, and exchanges the objects of sense for the ideas of Soul.
>
> These ideas are perfectly real and tangible to spiritual consciousness, and they have this advantage over the objects and thoughts of material sense—they are good and eternal.[6]

Mrs. Eddy's formulations no doubt were a response to the growth of the materialist perspectives in her time. Hers was a scheme of purification that would not allow the "mingling of good and evil." Her rhetoric was unqualified argument for the healing power made possible through union of self with the spiritual—the Divine Principle. Even so, her concept of these beliefs as a "science of being" merged a material referent with a spiritual one. Perhaps she did this to give her doctrine some of the ethos of the newly heralded physical sciences. Like physical science, Mrs. Eddy's methods sought control over the material elements of being.

Mrs. Eddy's use of spiritual–material division dramatically shows the inevitably dialectical nature of the terms of the *topos*. Christian Science doctrine makes the ultimate claim for the spiritual: it is real and the material is unreal. It is well known that this doctrine has appealed especially to those who suffer from physical afflictions. Whatever the empirical value of such beliefs, we must ask what rhetorically motivates such identifications.

According to Mrs. Eddy, evidence of the material is found only in corrupted perception. Yet from a strictly rhetorical point of view, Mrs. Eddy's argument depends entirely on the perceived reality of material loss. Without this perception there would be no need for the healing power of identification with the spiritual. Furthermore, as her argument is developed, perception of the material is the locus and cause of suffering in the world. The unhealthiness of the material is the motivation for seeking a "scientific" remedy in identification with the purely spiritual. This identification, Mrs. Eddy's doctrine says, brings miraculous transformation of what was formerly erroneously perceived: illness, material failure, and the like.

Christian Science rhetoric offers an unusually clear instance of rhetoric that urges transformation as the basis for transcendence. Whether or not actual transformation of physical malady ever occurs is irrelevant to the doctrine, for in denying the reality of the material one can transcend physical suffering.

Mrs. Eddy's explicit formulation of spiritual–material conflict points to the dialectical necessity of having a dualistic framework for rhetorical motivation toward change. Absolute denial of one term or the other would deny any rhetor means of arguing the fallibility of one term or superiority of the other. Recommendations for change are necessarily based upon locating problems and finding solutions. This requires that both terms be posited. Thus, the back cover of a current edition of *Science and Health* claims one may overcome material losses such as "business reverses and family strife," "drug use," or want of a "fulfilled sense of identity." These are contemporary maladies unlikely to have been prominent in Mrs. Eddy's thoughts as she wrote her book, but it is today claimed they can be cured by the same immersion in the spiritual that allows one to "feel God's power in the healing of sickness," the more traditional claim of Christian Science. Like contemporary therapies, present-day Christian Science offers transformation of our participation in the material world—in business, family, drugs, and, notably, identity. Even if belief fails to transform the material reality, belief has the power of transforming one's self through identification with the spiritual. And the spiritual is defined as the only real element of world. Any feeling of material loss is then only evidence that the individual has failed to accomplish full spiritual understanding and identification. Thus, material failures are transformed by the rhetoric into spiritual failures, for which there is a solution in study and faith.

Mrs. Eddy's dichotomization of the spiritual and material is hierarchically absolute. Both are elevated to the status of universal orders, and together they cover all sensate and intellectual experience. The individual is identified with both orders of being; his or her participation in both is humanly inevitable. The two orders are given absolute evaluative status as good and evil. So is an individual's identification and participation in these orders. Without a person's active purification of self through total identification with the spiritual, his or her world is a house divided, what James described as a divided self. Importantly, even though the material is "unreal" in doctrine, the spiritual life must be *chosen;* "the discords of corporeal sense must yield to the harmony of spiritual sense," else failure and disease become our lot. Mrs. Eddy's formulations appear extreme, but her "science" is completely consistent with the basic tropism of religious rhetoric. Her rhetoric also reflects James's analysis of the existential plight of the religious seeker: "There are two lives, the natural and the spiritual, and we must lose the one before we can participate in the other."[7]

I cannot think it an accident that extreme formulations of spiritual purity and superiority such as Mrs. Eddy's and those examined by James should arise in the wake of Marxist and evolutionary thought, or that Mrs. Eddy should coopt the term "science" for her metaphysics. Mrs. Eddy's spiritualism is the exact opposite of Marx's materialism, though there is a similarity in their views of individual failure and incompletion. Marx preserved Hegel's dialectical design of spiritual–material forces, reversing the superior–subordinate positions of spiritual and material. He changed Hegel's analysis from a transcendent doctrine to a transformative one. Mrs. Eddy's dialectic might be viewed as a reversal of Marx's. In one sense she retained the transformative emphasis of Marx, yet in another sense her therapy is transcendent. Regardless of these emphases, there is remarkable dialectical similarity between Mrs. Eddy and Hegel, and remarkable similarity between Mrs. Eddy and Marx. This similarity is not only dialectical but rhetorical, as is easily seen in their ways of arguing for the superiority of either the spiritual or material. Marx also saw the cause of failure as essentially one of mistaken perceptions:

The production of ideas, of conceptions, of consciousness, is at first directly interwoven with the material activity and the material

118

intercourse of men, the language of real life. Conceiving, thinking, the mental intercourse of men, appear at this stage as the direct efflux of their material behavior. The same applies to mental production as expressed in the language of politics, laws, morality, religion, metaphysics, etc. of a people. . . . Consciousness can never be any else than conscious existence, and the existence of men is their actual life process. If in all ideology men and circumstances appear upside-down as in a *camera obscura*, this phenomenon arises just as much from their historical life-process as the inversion of objects on the retina does from their physical life process.[8]

Spiritual failure is for Marx the ground of claiming the superiority of the material and for positing material solutions to man's ills. For Mrs. Eddy, failure to recognize and address the spiritual is the fault that lies at the base of all maladies. In Marx, failure to recognize and address the fault of neglecting the material is at the base of all strife. For Mrs. Eddy, one's spiritual being is transformed to bring resolution to material strife. For Marx, spiritual being must ultimately be transformed to bring resolution to material strife. At some point, for both thinkers, spiritual and material must be brought into an ideal alignment so that the two realms are set in correct relationship and individual failure eliminated. In both cases, the rhetorical functions of the terms of the *topos* are the same despite the absolute contradiction in assigning superior status to the terms.

As I have suggested, one need not posit a total contradiction between spiritual and material in order to explain or cope with perceived failure. A third possibility exists and is frequently used. One can posit a balance or constructive interchange between the spiritual and material. In the intellectually troubled era of Marx and Mrs. Eddy, the third path was chosen as a way of coping with the apparent conflict between the spiritual–material bases of religion and science. In *Darwin in America*, Cynthia Russet points out that responses to evolutionary theory were not limited to challenges against the theory or against religion. The conflict between science and religion.

engendered all those theologies directly based upon evolutionary concepts, whose liberalizing influence in the way of softening the older Puritan doctrine extended beyond the relatively small circle of professed religious liberals. These theologies so identified evolution with moral and spiritual progress, with "God's way of doing things," that evolution in the natural world and redemption in the spiritual world could be viewed as analogous processes, with God resident at the center of both.[9]

Something of this sort can be seen in the speech by Gillies that Wilder placed at the turn of the century. Spiritual and material considerations can also be joined in ways that favor the material side without wholly obliterating the spiritual. I shall show shortly that Teilhard de Chardin attempted to do this. The evolutionary and biophysical metaphysics in vogue today also illustrate this way of handling the spiritual–material *topos*. The new physics has brought forth new hosts of priests and prophets offering hope that the physical structure of the universe will soon yield secrets that can create a new order and new spiritual values for humanity. As we have seen, Rifkin believed that perhaps this had been accomplished with entropy, while Skinner hoped for it in the behavioral sciences.

Whatever relationship is posited between spiritual and material forces, the relationship will become a basis for analyzing and resolving failure. It seems that the discussion of this relationship is in fact more basic than either self–society or past–future formulations, at least where spiritual-material matters are treated directly. Within the scaffolding of the spiritual–material dualism, one posits a structured universe. That structure is treated as an absolute and ubiquitous order. Ideas and actions are evaluated according to their consistency with the posited universal order. This is the method of determining shortcomings and successes. The universe, the order, and the evaluation are treated as having the qualities of continuity, predictability, and accountability. On the basis of this stable interpretation of the world, one determines the choices and actions that will make any self consistent with the ordered, inescapable system within which we live. This is the rhetorical shape and substance of any attempt to rectify human failure on the basis of spiritual–material considerations. It does not matter which side of the *topos* is favored or whether some intermix of the two paired forces is directly formulated; these are rhetorical functions that must be carried out and served in any comprehensive scheme of coping with failure.

THE UNIVERSE OF FAILURE

Even where failure has been defined and analyzed in terms of self–society, and even where an individual has interpreted and formulated solutions with the methods of past–future analysis, the *topos* spiritual-material will be resorted to if one completes therapeutic analysis and forges complete, and in some sense final methods of recovery. In this section I would like to explore how it is that spiritual–material themes serve in combination with the other *topoi* and how they may serve to reorder or reinterpret the other *topoi* in general treatments of human failure.

Of the *topoi* I have identified, spiritual–material is perhaps the most important for accomplishing the ends of compensation and consolation. Returning to the examples of self–society themes analyzed in chapter 4, one will see the spiritual–material *topos* featured even more prominently than the self–society. I chose these examples precisely to demonstrate that even where self–society is not an obvious theme, it must logically inhere in treatments of failure and assignments of responsibility. Here I wish to show that when failure is sorted out in terms of self–society and internalized as a problem for self, grounds are simultaneously established for treating failure in *spiritual–material* terms. As the thinkers I discussed worked through the problems of self–society and composed rationales according to past–future considerations, they came upon their complete and comprehensive solutions by developing a spiritual–material division and reunification.

The same is true of the examples of dealing with time that I presented in chapter 5. When people review past experience and future expectations, and impose temporal or nontemporal (transcendent) orders accordingly, they establish grounds for considering failure, self, and world in spiritual–material terms. As my examples of past–future themes suggested, when individuals seek eternal or transcendent grounds for treating failure and imbue those grounds with transformative possibilities, they inevitably draw their ideas from contemplation of spiritual–material themes and characterizations. To treat failures in complete and comprehensive ways, spiritual–material themes are needed to establish transcendent and transformative grounds for resolving failures *in principle*. Spiritual–material themes serve to complete the healing process by giving persons general explanations and treatments that become guides for living and sources of consolation and compensation for any and all failures in the future.

My earlier examples help to illustrate James's claim that religious discourse is but one species of a genus of therapeutic patterns. To show further how spiritual–material treatments can resolve problems found in self–social and past–future relations, I wish now to examine a pair of essentially philosophical writers. These authors' uses of spiritual–material themes are interesting variations on those of traditional religious discourse.

121

Pierre Teilhard de Chardin and Ralph Waldo Emerson composed schemes for treating human failure in universal terms. Their world views were religiously radical because each sought to reverse or reform standard patterns of religious thought and interpretation. Both men focused on failure as a natural principle of human life, and both saw in failure the wellspring of human spiritual growth. Their therapeutic rhetorics follow the essential pattern that James sketched, despite the fact that they posited spiritual–material relations almost directly opposed to the religious doctrines they sought to reform.

Teilhard de Chardin was a twentieth-century Jesuit scholar whose entire work addresses the chasm he believed exists between the spiritual and material realms of human experience. He sought to bridge this chasm by constructing a metaphysic of human experience wherein spiritual and material dimensions are so profoundly related that all human failure is diminished. Teilhard was a geologist by inclination and education, and his studies were preoccupied with the material world and with evolutionary history. Nonetheless he saw his study as a spiritual pursuit, and he probed the material world for its meanings about creation, human development, and the significance of human life. As a spiritual man, he tried to justify his concentration on the material world—a concentration sometimes intensely disapproved of by the Church. Teilhard faced the deep philosophical and religious separation of spiritual and material matters that has for centuries been fundamental to Christian thought. In his writings he undertook to infuse our understanding of the material world with the spiritual values of religious thought, and so to retain the unity of his concept of God.

The grand unification of spiritual and material processes came to Teilhard in an inspirational concept of growth. He believed that this basic process in the universe ultimately brings divisive elements together into one consistent whole. He wrote that "from the smallest individual detail to the vastest aggregations, our living universe (in common with our inorganic universe) has a structure, and this structure can owe its nature only to a phenomenon of growth."[10] Consoling as a unity through growth may be, Teilhard's formulation of the meaning and implications of this unity proceeded by means of the compensatory *topoi*. Unlike most spiritualists, he wished to defend the material, future, and individual elements in life as meaningful parts of the larger scheme of things.

Teilhard's search in the physical unity of the universe for the grounds of consolation led him to understand consolation as one massive compensation that God makes for the reality of human diminishment;—we are diminished by the overwhelming forces of the physical universe.

122

Teilhard makes this clear by portraying God's motives as compensatory, in that he will make good all human loss in the future:

> In virtue of his very perfections, God cannot ordain that the elements of a world in the course of growth—or at least of a fallen world in the process of rising again—should avoid shocks and diminishments, even moral ones: *necessarium est ut scandala eveniant*. But God will make it good—he will take his revenge, if one may use the expression—by making evil itself serve a higher good of his faithful, the very evil which the present state of creation does not allow him to suppress immediately.[11]

Teilhard's understanding of the ways God uses failure is expressed from a consolatory position containing definite material referents:

> Like an artist who is able to make use of a fault or an impurity in the stone he sculpting or the bronze he is casting so as to produce more exquisite lines or a more beautiful tone, God, without sparing us the partial deaths, nor the final death, which form an essential part of our lives, transfigures them by integrating them in a better plan.[12]

This is a scheme of compensation, where vicissitudes are transfigured into a product that is better than before, where all fault and suffering, including death, are part of a process of improvement. Again, this scheme of compensation allows for the integrity of the individual, the future erasure of failure, and material purity. The *topoi* of consolation are implicit: there is a special sense in which the collective integration of individuals, the meaning of past failures, and the ordainments of the spiritual operate as a unity in this scheme. Ultimately all the *topoi* of failure are integrated and all divisions dissolved in a grand compensatory operation, the understanding of which gives us the therapeutic grounds for consolation in the present.

Teilhard addressed failure in individual, futuristic, and material terms:

> Providence, for those who believe in it, converts evil into good in three principal ways. Sometimes the check we have undergone will divert our activity on to objects, or towards a framework, that are more propitious—though still situated on the level of the human ends we are pursuing [compensation]. . . . At other times, more often perhaps, the loss which afflicts us will oblige us to turn for the satisfaction of our frustrated desires to less material fields,

which neither worm nor rust can corrupt [consolation]. . . . Failure in that case plays for us the part that the elevator plays for an aircraft or the pruning knife for a plant. It canalises the sap of our inward life, disengages the purest "components" of our being in such a way as to make us shoot up higher and straighter. The collapse, even when a moral one, is thus transformed into a success which, however spiritual it may be is, nevertheless, felt *experimentally.*[13]

Even Teilhard's idea of consolation and spirituality is here cast in material terms and as a material process of growth, actualized "experimentally" and transformed in material reality. The spiritual grounds of consolation appear to be insufficient for Teilhard, and his analysis seeks to demonstrate that consolation for human failure is individual, material, and, of course, to be actualized in a guaranteed future resolution.

The *topoi* used in these passages indicate the compensatory nature of Teilhard's metaphysics. Yet it is clear that Teilhard believed that these principles, fully understood, provided a complete response to the problem of human failing. There are human losses—such as the death of infants—that seem to be incompensable, but Teilhard's compensatory logic was so universal that it addressed even these failures, and showed how God transfigures such suffering:

How can these diminishments which are altogether without compensation, wherein we see death at its most deathly, become for us a good? This is where we can see the third way in which Providence operates in the domain of our diminishments—the most effective way and the way which most surely makes us holy.

God, as we have seen, has already transfigured our sufferings by making them serve our conscious fulfillment. In his hands the forces of diminishment have perceptibly become the tool that cuts, carves and polishes within us the stone which is destined to occupy a definite place in the heavenly Jerusalem.[14]

The ultimate compensation for suffering and loss is this divine transfiguration; the soul is being fitted for its place in heaven. Spiritual development is created by pains and failings that defy our normal understanding and seem incompensable.

In more orthodox Christian views, such mysteries are either punishments or tests of faith that one must endure without loss of faith. One's faith and its intensification become consolation for such suffering, and one is compensated ultimately by God's grace and salvation. Teilhard has

rendered this orthodox function, not in terms of spiritual faith and consolation, but in terms of compensation: these failures and pains are sys-
tematically constructive; they perfect the individual and his or her
material suffering through transfiguration into a future state of divinity.

Religion has always used evidences of inevitable suffering and failure
as proof of the need for spiritual consolation. The same spiritual end can
be met, Teilhard seemed to argue, by a fuller understanding of the ways
of compensation and the meanings of the material. By giving the material a universal status, his idea of universal compensation fulfills the
function of consolation. As in standard Christian formulas, we are re-
paid in death for the travail of life. Yet Teilhard had in a sense reversed
our standard interpretation of the consolatory process. The process is
compensatory, but he transformed the end—death—into a collective,
eternal, spiritual condition:

> God must, in some way or other, make room for himself, hollow-
> ing us out and emptying us, if he is finally to penetrate into us.
> And in order to assimilate us in him, he must break the molecules
> of our being so as to re-cast and re-model us. The function of
> death is to provide the necessary entrance into our inmost selves. It
> will make us undergo the required dissociation. It will put us into
> the state organically needed if the divine fire is to descend upon us.
> And in that way its fatal power to decompose and dissolve will be
> harnessed to the most sublime operations of life.[15]

Here eternity and spiritual being are not used in the standard ways of
consoling for death; they do not transcend, but they transform death.
The physical and material are not denied but decomposed; our "mole-
cules" are broken for the purpose of "re-casting" us. One is not drawn
from the material realm upward toward the light; rather, the light de-
scends upon one and transforms. One does not shed the physical bonds
of life, but the physical bonds are part of a temporal process of decom-
position and dissolution that allows spirit to enter and occupy the material world. One does not abandon one's material self to enter a spiritual
domain; one's material self is the logically and temporally prior condition for the spiritual to become immanent in the material world.

In Teilhard's therapeutic scheme the *topoi* of compensation are universal principles. At this universal level they are integrated into a view
which encompasses all human failure. From these principles the grounds
for consolation are readily drawn. For Teilhard and any follower, all
failure would be ultimately resolvable and, in Teilhard's word, "reconcil-

able" by resort to the interpretations that are here possible. Teilhard's therapy accomplishes precisely the same functions as traditional Christian doctrine, and it produces a different yet compatible perspective even while using the opposite *topoi*. This is done by spiritualizing the material, collectivizing the individual in a view of humankind that preserves individuality, and interpreting the future in such a way that the future is the logical and necessary unfolding of the past. Teilhard's rhetoric is therefore appealing to those with individualistic, materialistic, and futuristic orientations—a good description of a contemporary audience—and perhaps to those drawn readily to a compensatory logic. In Teilhard's universal scheme, all failures are readily compensated and consoled by the larger picture. If the scheme were followed completely, there would never be a need to choose between strategies of consolation and compensation. But Teilhard arrived at this scheme by emphasizing the *topoi* of compensation, which places human failure in a new perspective, one that is unusual in Christian thought.

In Ralph Waldo Emerson's essay on "Compensation" there is a similar yet somewhat opposite dialectical move. Emerson articulates what he calls the law of compensation, a law that so universalizes the consolatory that it produces an ultimately compensatory approach to all human failure. Emerson's move is less a spiritualization of the material than an attempt to materialize the spiritual.

Emerson is remembered for his emphasis on individualism and nature and for the school of transcendentalism with which he is identified. In "Compensation" he took traditional materialist interpretations of life and showed their spiritual basis. The common idea of redemption was his point of departure: "Ever since I was a boy, I have wished to write a discourse on Compensation: for, it seemed to me when very young, that, on this subject life was ahead of theology, and the people knew more than the preachers taught." He continued:

> I was lately confirmed in these desires by hearing a sermon at church. The preacher, a man esteemed for his orthodoxy, unfolded in the ordinary manner the doctrine of the Last Judgment. He assumed that judgment is not executed in this world; that the wicked are successful; that the good are miserable; and then urged from reason and from Scripture a compensation to be made to both parties in the next life.[16]

Here is the traditional Christian duality between the spiritual and the material realms. Material suffering encountered in this life is compensated through reward in the next, and material success in this life is apt to be ground for condemnation in the next. The idea of redemption itself is a case of spiritualizing the material, for it is literally an economic term, a "buying back," that has been appropriated to express a spiritual consolation for suffering and a material kind of punishment for wrong-doing.

This conception of redemption particularly disturbed Emerson and led him to question the idea that compensation is made in the afterlife:

> Was it that houses and lands, offices, wine, horses, luxury, are had by unprincipled men, whilst the saints are poor and despised; and that a compensation is to be made to these last hereafter, by giving them life gratifications another day—bank stock and doubloons, venison and champagne? This must be the compensation intended, for what else?[17]

Emerson pointed up the fact that the orthodox Christian idea of redemption, often used to console for earthly failures, is really an idea of compensation. He showed that this conception of redemption is based on compensatory *topoi*, in that it promises some individual, future, and material sort of reward. Emerson countered this idea of compensation by suggesting that actual compensation belongs to a different order of things, and that compensatory reward is not only in the future but in the present and the past as well. His version of spiritual recompense transcends the materiality of experience. This is precisely the structure of consolation; spirituality displaces materiality as the individual participates in and understands the higher nature of experience. Emerson's imagery was compensatory, but his compensation, like that of Teilhard, was consoling.

Consider Emerson's discussion of human labor as the model for compensation:

> Human labor, through all of its forms, from the sharpening of a stake to the construction of a city or an epic, is one immense illustration of the perfect compensation of the universe. The absolute balance of Give and Take, the doctrine that everything has its price,—and if that price is not paid, not that thing but something else is obtained, and that it is impossible to get anything without its price,—is not less sublime in the columns of a le[d]ger than in the budgets of states, in the laws of light and darkness, in all the action and reaction of nature.[18]

Emerson's example and his language derived from the material side of the spiritual–material *topos;* yet labor was given spiritual dimensions and significance. Labor and its rewards, for which people usually expect compensation, were universalized to "all the action and reaction of nature." Nothing we can conceive of is not "give and take," paying a price and receiving what was paid for. So broadly conceived, labor enacts spiritual ideas and values in the material world. Labor builds, molds, and shapes the world, and when done spiritually, this shaping accords with spiritual ideals and nature's universal laws.

Emerson's discourse faithfully executed the material idea of compensation and used the appropriate *topoi.* But when he abstracted a law and doctrine from the principle of compensation, he spiritualized it, made it universal, and drew all of human experience under its domain. He tried to demonstrate that the balancing and reparational principle of compensation is not just the substitution of one thing for another, an exchange; the spiritual dominates the material as it compensates for material faults and losses. In our knowledge of this domination, certified by law, there is consolation.

Emerson infused nature with spiritual meaning throughout his writings, and he emphasized the collective soul, though he treated it as an extension of individual souls. This spiritualization and collectivization appeared in his portrayal of spiritual benefits—still in economic terms:

> The same guards which protect us from disaster, defect, and enmity, defend us, if we will, from selfishness and fraud. Bolts and bars are not the best of our institutions, nor is shrewdness in trade a mark of wisdom. Men suffer all their life long, under the foolish superstition that they can be cheated. But it is as impossible for a man to be cheated by any one but himself, as for a thing to be, and not be, at the same time. There is a third silent party to all our bargains. The nature and soul of things takes on itself the guaranty of the fulfillment of every contract, so that honest service cannot come to a loss. If you serve an ungrateful master, serve him the more. Put God in your debt. Every stroke shall be repaid. The longer the payment is withholden, the better for you; for compound interest is the rate and usage of this exchequer.[19]

This has the sound of compensation, but the reader is not really given anything to "balance." The material world and its values are seen as outweighed and dominated by the "third silent party." This is a spiritual compensation that is of a different order from ordinary pay for labor. Suffering is paid off, with interest, by grace. Emerson pursued the goal of compensation to the point of making loss an impossibility. One's spiritual benefits accrue in compounded proportion to one's efforts and suffering. But the mark of consolation is here; there is a substitution of one set of values for another: "The martyr cannot be dishonored. Every lash inflicted is a tongue of fame; every prison a more illustrious abode; every burned book or house enlightens the world; every suppressed or expunged word reverberates through the earth from side to side." While it is made to sound as though all of these losses are compensated directly, the topical moves of consolation are present. The sacrificed self can be consoled by fame; tragedies and perversions of justice are consoled by faith in a higher court; the reader can reconstruct the past by imbuing its suffering with new meanings; one's social participation and spiritual self are rescued.

That Emerson rhetorically altered his initial idea of a perfectly balanced compensation is clear when he begins his exposition of the soul thus:

> There is a deeper fact in the soul than compensation, to wit, its own nature. The soul is not a compensation, but a life. The soul *is.* Under all this running sea of circumstances, whose waters ebb and flow with perfect balance, lies the aboriginal abyss of real Being. Essence, or God, is not a relation, or a part, but the whole. Being is the vast affirmative, excluding negation, self-balanced, and swallowing up all relations, parts and times, within itself.[20]

The real balance thus lies beyond the material world. A unity and wholeness of being swallows up all earthly events and meanings into an "aboriginal abyss." Emerson is expressing the ultimate unity of material things with spirit. Like Teilhard de Chardin, he located God and love as the sources of consolatory and compensatory power. Unlike Teilhard, who saw this ultimate unity of spirit and matter as transforming human failure, Emerson found in the ultimate unity transcendence of all human failure. This difference, I believe, is the ultimate difference between a compensatory solution and a consolatory solution to the problem of failure.

Emerson, like Teilhard, took one reparational goal and abstracted its therapeutic rationale into a comprehensive perspective on all failure, error, and loss. At such a level of universalization the grounds for both compensation and consolation are present, and it is thus easy to account for and resolve any failure. In his final transcendent move from the universal soul he has posited, Emerson used the *topoi* of consolation to

129

complete his account. In his grand scheme the individual finds resolution within a transcendent collective as "the heart and soul of all men being one, this bitterness of *His* and *Mine* ceases. He is mine. I am my brother and my brother is me."[21] From this vantage point all "mountainous inequalities vanish." Emerson saw the ultimate resolution of human strife in understanding, rather than in action or material transformation. The "compensations of calamity are made apparent to the understanding." Such a compensation comes from a spiritual understanding that allows one to reorganize the past and put any failure in a new perspective. That is the goal of consolation. Failure is not erased nor balanced, but "in the nature of the soul is the compensation for the inequalities of condition." Emerson's dialectical argument thus proceeded from the logic of compensation and, by rhetorical interpretations of the *topoi* of compensation, wound up articulating the perfect consolation.

We are identified with the world around us in such ways that problems in the world can appear failures for us as individuals. Emerson and Teilhard undertook to solve the problem of human inadequacy by reinterpreting the identifications and relationships of human identity and the world. They sought to do so within the framework of Christian thought, but by changing this thought to accommodate new or what they believed were more realistic assessments of individuals' relationships to the world. In essence, they were functioning as rhetoricians, adapting the persuasive goals of traditional spirituality to solve pressing problems of identification.

Teilhard and Emerson both preserve individualism in their spirituality, they both see in nature a model for the spiritual order, and they both use compensatory *topoi* to characterize the individual's place in this order. Yet their arguments move quite differently toward similar ends. Teilhard sought to show how the ultimate scheme of compensation could fulfill the same goals as the consolatory logic of traditional Catholicism; he focused on the powers of the spiritual to transform the material. Emerson sought to show how practical compensation in the world mandates that we ultimately accept the traditional grounds of consolatory logic. The evidences of materiality, properly understood, can only lead to the necessity of the spiritual. This is a doctrine of transcendence. Teilhard asserted the unity of the essential self with God. Emerson asserted the ultimately benign governance of nature. It is because of the total identification of self with God (spirit) or with nature (spiritualized order) that Teilhard's compensatory model consoles and Emerson's consolatory model compensates.

Each writer drew lines of thought and characterization from all three of what I call the *topoi* of coping with failure. Each presupposed an apparent division between imperfect individual selves and society. Each viewed past and present perceptions of human experience as the problem, and each offered an orientation toward the future that would solve that problem if individuals changed their perceptions of their own identities. To compose and articulate these universal schemes of treating failure, both men resorted to the themes and formulae of the spiritual–material *topos*. That is to say, too, that resort to the spiritual–material topos allowed them to solve the inherent conflicts of self–society and past–future. Teilhard produced a way of transforming failure in the future, and Emerson produced a way of transcending failure through reconsideration of what past failures mean. Ultimately, and most fundamentally, each author struggled with the dialectical relations of the material and the spiritual, abstracting and universalizing the qualities of each to produce a unification of the two. With either scheme of unification, all failures of self or society and all failures of past or future can be compensated and consoled.

THE VARIETIES OF RHETORICAL EXPERIENCE

Whenever we talk about spiritual and material aspects of a phenomenon, we do more than assert the dialectical relationship of the two concepts and more than contrast their characteristics in what we say. We also spiritualize or materialize the concepts we deal with. Even when we claim that the material is the superior or determinative order and force, we spiritualize the material order by treating it as something incorporeal. Likewise, when we express the superiority and power of the spiritual and point to evidences of that superiority in the world, we materialize the spiritual by citing sensible, tangible, proofs of its superiority. Teilhard and Emerson provide examples of where all materiality could, rhetorically, be spiritualized and where all spirituality could be rhetorically materialized in the evidences of corporeal life. Whenever we discuss the spiritual–material qualities of anything, we claim and argue about the most fundamental qualities Western culture conceives of. Whatever other qualities an action or phenomenon has derive from the spiritual–material qualities of the action or phenomenon. In sum, the dialectical relations of spirituality and materiality overarch all other relations, at least as Western culture portrays the world.

I contend that a world view that permits rhetorical address as a legitimate way of dealing with experience must have some fundamental spiritual–material orientations, because rhetorical address is itself a way of reconciling or conjoining the spiritual and material. That is, to hold that rhetoric is necessary, legitimate, or effective in solving problems, one must implicitly hold that the material world can be influenced by ideas that draw significance from some spiritualized order, and that spiritualized ideas can be materialized in word and deed. All rhetorical treatments of human failing and human betterment must posit criteria for success and failure. This inevitably requires that some material conditions have spiritual significance, that intellect or cognition can give order to the conditions, and that some spiritualized causes or outcomes can be materialized in the world of things. The cult of material success, so prevalent in America today, is a good example. As long as success is placed at the pinnacle among values, the arguments for it must attribute spiritual accomplishment to its attainment. We even see and hear religious testimony that spirituality has brought success in business, career, or sports, thereby making material success the marker and goal of spiritual correctness.

I am asserting that whenever anyone undertakes to analyze the experience of failure through rhetoric, and sorts out or reconstructs that failure so that remedial responses are possible, he or she necessarily becomes involved with the spiritual–material analysis on which that rhetoric is based. Even through contemplation of self–society or past–future themes one will discover how self or society, or past or future have been spiritualized or materialized in connotation. Considered in the abstract, these *topoi* arise from some basic spiritual–material analysis. Spiritual–material themes enter rhetorical usage whenever anyone needs to generalize his or her theory of the failure, assign relative values to options, or be assured that his or her response to this failure will conform with some valued pattern or order of things.

I suggest that *rhetorical experience* is the genus of psychological remedy that James found illustrated in religious expression. When people engage in therapeutic rhetoric, they must somehow believe that: (1) there is the potential for division or conflict between spiritual life and material being; (2) this potential for disunion should be remedied through establishing and maintaining a "proper" relationship between spiritual and material; (3) discourse—rhetoric—can evoke and display remedial relations between spiritual and material realms of life. I contend that these ontological premises operate whenever rhetoric is used therapeutically. These premises may operate for the speaker or for the hearer alone, or they may be the shared premises of the discourse.

Considered practically, uses of spiritual–material themes involve two rhetorical strategies that enable people to explain and weigh the data of experience: (1) one may spiritualize items, events, situations, and action by portraying them as parts and products of spiritual influence; (2) one may materialize concepts, essences, and ideas normally associated with the spiritual by pointing to their manifestations in material experiences. Rhetorical stress on the material can yield spiritualization, and stress on the spiritual can yield unique conceptions of the material. For instance, although Marx's materialism posits that the material is the basis for all order and value, his perspective ironically leads to criteria for spiritual success. In his argument the material world is spiritualized as the means for fulfillment of all human spiritual goals. This is also true in the iconoclastic materialism of behavioral science. There the elevation of the material engenders aesthetic and moral criteria for judging knowledge, social virtue, and individual action. As Teilhard and Emerson illustrate, the two strategies can be conjoined, so that manifestations of both spiritual and material dimensions are seen in a given item or idea. This done, one can offer an interpretation that demonstrates both the spiritual significance of a material phenomenon and the material presence of spiritual value. The rhetorical strategies of spiritualizing matter and of materializing spirit are thus instrumental in therapeutic rhetoric. Both are necessary to achieve symbolic transformation and transcendence in human experience.

Operations of rhetoric in Western culture presume a spiritual–material analysis that all who engage in rhetoric implicitly share. Our culture embraces a fundamental spiritual–material dualism as the cause of human problems, and it also embraces rhetorical exercise as a viable way of solving human problems. Although they may appear to be extreme, the formulations of Mrs. Eddy, Marx, Hegel, theological evolutionism, and evolutionary cosmology are expressions of this traditional Western dualism. These systems draw upon the pervasive traditions of Christianity, Western philosophy, and science. Even though Teilhard and Emerson sought to reform interpretations of this tradition radically, they did so *through* spiritual–material analysis, not by challenging the essential perception of spiritual–material dualism. In the context of Western tradition, the spiritual–material themes used by all of these thinkers are typical. In addition, people in Western cultures have not only these traditions but dramatic and folkloric notions of fate, magic, and supernaturalism that inform their ordinary interpretations of experience, as is also true in other cultures. At least as they are practiced in the West, these traditions also reflect basic spiritual–material themes.

The conception of spiritual–material dualism and the power of rhetoric to heal or resolve this dualism is thus traditional and seemingly fundamental in Western culture. This tradition is indicated in Plato's formulation of the power of the spiritual: Diotima tells Socrates that love is a *daimon,* a power which

> interprets and conveys to the gods the prayers and sacrifices of men, and to men the commands and rewards of the gods; and this power spans the chasm which divides them, and in this all is bound together, and through this the arts of the prophet and the priest, their sacrifices and mysteries and charms, and all prophecy and incantation, find their way. For God mingles not with man; and through this power all the intercourse and speech of God with man, whether awake or asleep, is carried on.[22]

Plato alludes primarily to the religious power and the poetic functions of discourse. But in terms of the healing power of rhetoric and its function to bridge or unify the sense of spiritual–material duality and conflict, we may, like James, assume that other species of rhetorical expression also carry these psychological underpinnings.

Uses of spiritual–material themes are easily observed in everyday experience. A fisherman comes home empty-handed and ascribes his material lot to "luck." Automobile and airplane accidents are understood as "God's will" or part of "God's plan." "Acts of God" still figure in many insurance policies as a special kind of cause of fault. Scholars attribute complexities of material developments and causes to a mysterious and invisible "zeitgeist" that operates in the world. Many religions hold out the possibility of miracles that materially reveal spiritual force. Most people still cling to some sense of "fate," implying that they believe spiritual and material forces cooperate in determining human outcomes. Most people also still retain some sense of "magic," implying that spiritual and material forces interact to transform at least *human* reality. In the concepts of "war," "society," "economy," "capitalism," "communism," "credit," "debt," "technology," "nature," "progress," "tradition," "achievement," "development," "sacrifice," and "consumption," material events in the world are given spiritualized order and purpose, and our participation in those events gives spiritual significance to our material being.

Logically or ontologically, one can argue that the perception of failure implies some discrepancy between spiritual goals and material actualization, as I showed in the first portion of this book. One can argue, as I have in this chapter, that rhetoric itself relies on some fundamental belief that spiritual ideas or goals can be actualized in the material world. It follows, therefore, that any address to human problems will imply that individuals have failed to manifest spiritual–material order properly, and

134

that some therapeutic benefit of self-unity will be had in performing or completing actions recommended or by manifesting "correct" beliefs.

Thematic treatments of self and world in terms of spiritual–material division and merger are involved in rhetorical expression at the most fundamental level. Evidence of this can be found by examining basic rhetorical views of language and rhetorical practices. The common concept of god-terms in rhetorical theory refers to a practice of using connotatively charged, evaluative terms to express "goods." The use of such terms invokes a certain character of the world, it implies some kind of order at work, and it assigns value to the items or ideas to which the terms are applied. A god-term or a devil-term is a symbol that expresses a spiritual–material union that has been established in rhetorical experience of audiences. The use of such a term indicates that a general scheme for universalizing, ordering, and evaluating experience has been worked out, and is shared by speaker and audience.

Terms such as I have listed—"economy," "capitalism," "credit," "fate," "justice," and the like—function as common god- and devil-terms in rhetorical exchanges. Such terms summarize the metaphysical dimensions of alignments and values and ways of solving problems. Teilhard's universal scheme advanced the transformative and transcendent powers of "love" and "growth," as did Emerson's use of "labor," "soul," and "compensation." In short, such terms can be used to represent concepts where spiritual and material relations are disjoined or harmonized.

Uses of god- and devil-terms recur in rhetorical practice. The psychological processes associated with their use are suggested in Rollo May's treatment of "Psychotherapy and the Daimonic." May affirms that self-division and treatment of problems in a "universal" language are central features of healing processes involving self-persuasion. He writes:

> The daimonic in an individual pushes him toward the logos. That is to say, the more I come to terms with my daimonic tendencies, the more I will find myself living by a universal structure of reality. The logos in this sense is transpersonal. We saw that the daimonic begins as impersonal. But by deepening my consciousness I make my daimonic tendencies personal. We move thus from an impersonal through a personal to a transpersonal dimension.[23]

May was dealing with straightforward cases of self-division and daimonic symbolization by persons in extreme psychological distress. We may say, however, that this same process of "living by a universal structure of reality" is invoked whenever god- and devil-terms imply that such a universal structure is real. Such terms and their connotations are rhetorical ways of personalizing conflicts in the world. They imply that transpersonal patterns exist for personal evaluations and means of coping. God-terms and devil-terms summarize and make immanent universal spiritual–material relations that people have worked out through rhetorical practice.

Kenneth Burke analyzed the uses of "money" and "technology" as god-terms in American culture.[24] As he showed, these terms reflect spiritual–material relations that Americans have worked out in ways that allow values to be summarily assigned when the terms are used. The concept "money" allows for both a spiritual expression of material involvement and for a material expression of spiritual involvement. Spiritual goals, ideals, and values can be subordinated to the material dimension of money, hence money can become a god-term for a spiritual leader who hopes to build a new church, create great art, or send a child to college. Likewise, our material efforts in labor, business, and production can be understood in their spiritual dimensions, as Emerson did in his view of labor. "Money" can be used to reduce all material effort to a symbolic currency that is capable of actualizing spiritual ideals, hence the material becomes spiritualized. "Technology" as a concept or term can also be used endow material involvements with spiritual value or to reduce spiritual values to material actuality. The rhetorical use of the concept can be a way of realizing spiritual ideas and goals in the material world, and a way of spiritualizing material pursuits and progress.

Richard Weaver saw in the concept of progress the great god-term of the modern age. It too can signify that spiritual advancement is attained through material accomplishment; and when we use the term, we spiritualize the material reality we describe as progress. For all of its material valence, "progress" seemed to Weaver "probably the only term which gives to the average American or West European of today a concept of something bigger than himself, which he is socially impelled to accept and even sacrifice for." Burke would no doubt agree with Weaver that "the capacity to demand sacrifice is probably the surest indicator of the 'god term.' "[25] As a concept, sacrifice implies that material being has spiritual significance because through sacrifice of the material the spiritual is somehow served.

Burke and Weaver also described the ways such terms function to invoke a world that has been structured by spiritual–material analysis. Burke wrote that "in any term we posit a world, in the sense that we can treat the world in terms of it, seeing all as emanations, near or far, of its light."[26] This, of course, describes the kind of rhetorical orientation that

James's religious seekers brought themselves to by observing their spiritual-material formulations, and it implies the daimonic functions that May spoke of. Weaver's explanation of god-terms clearly reveals the therapeutic rationale of these processes:

> By "god term" we mean that expression about which all other expressions are ranked as subordinate and serving dominations and powers. Its force imparts to the others their lesser degree of force, and fixes the scale by which degrees of comparison are understood. . . . It is the nature of the conscious life of man to revolve around some concept of value. So true is this that when the concept is withdrawn, or when it is forced into competition with another concept, the human being suffers an almost intolerable sense of being lost. He has to know where he is in the ideological cosmos in order to coordinate his activities. Probably the greatest cruelty which can be inflicted upon the psychic man is this deprivation of a sense of tendency.[27]

Weaver, like Burke, was trying to articulate the dialectical–rhetorical processes whereby an orienting and therapeutically significant connection is made between self and the dominant concepts of one's world view. Labels for those concepts become sacred, even for the advocate of materialism, because they are expressions of order and evaluation that impart their power of domination to other categories and lesser extensions of the terms. Such terms may be universalized, absolutized, and purified, and guidelines for interpretation and participation in the world can be drawn from them. Out of such hierarchical orders come valuative terms by means of which self and whatever is external to it will be measured. The process, as Burke noted, is tautological, for things of like value are attributed the same structure and function, and things of the same structure and function are given like evaluations.

Evaluative force in language is at the very heart of rhetorical exchange. Meaningful action and meaning itself seem quite impossible without some notion of value. What Burke, Weaver, and James were trying to express was that an individual completes his or her meaningful identification with the world at the level of common value (both good and bad), and that at bare minimum this is necessary for individual identity. What needs further expression is that values always grow from and are active in spiritual and material involvements. This is why discourse can move between spiritual and material structures without disrupting or changing the essential hierarchical order, and why in rhetorical function spiritualist and materialist doctrines appear to be

137

mirror images. Their value hierarchies remain fixedly opposed to one another.

God-terms are selected and empowered because they have the connotation of spiritual–material unity. They are expressions in which spirit and matter can be seen in conjoined, potentially harmonious relations. The god-terms of a society or group reflect spiritual–material unities that have already been worked out, so the term can indicate a widely accepted remedy for spiritual–material conflict. The dialectical character of consolation and compensation requires that we move between the spiritual and material aspects of things and ideas when we deal with failures. Interpretations and value assignments must remain consistent when we do this. The fact that a god-term invokes a structured spiritual–material relationship familiar to an audience's interpretations allows for such movement to take place.

The spiritual–material *topos* is integral to the workings of rhetoric even where the terms of the *topos* are not explicitly evoked, analyzed, or aligned. Rhetorical exchange is normally grounded in metaphysical concerns that guide treatments of spiritual–material address. The evaluative dimension of rhetorical language implies a perceived order of good and bad, positive or negative, and this order in turn implies some general or universal scheme or structure in the world. These schemes and structures are rendered explicit by using themes that are subsumed under the *topos* spiritual–material. As I have illustrated, we find scientific, philosophical, cultural, and religious rhetoric all addressing phenomena and concerns in terms of the spiritual–material.

The anchorings of one's metaphysical being in spiritual–material formulations provide options for transcendent beliefs and transformative actions by means of which one can manage experiences of failure. Such options must be exercised in therapeutic rhetoric precisely because one must prevent one's spiritual or material involvements from being wholly destroyed by a failure. When individuals are not able to sort through their experiences effectively in order to participate in normal spiritual–material involvements, we call them schizophrenic. For most persons, however, spiritual and material lives can be simultaneously maintained and in a fashion balanced. The function of therapeutic rhetoric is to discover and reveal how this can be done. Even the most thoroughgoing materialist must proceed with assurance that there is some spiritualized value and guidance in his or her plans and actions. Even the most devoted spiritualist must somehow reconcile to material life and believe that his or her actions materially express the spiritual values he or she holds as basic. In sum, we must be able to sort the data of experience,

138

weigh their relative value, and maintain some consistency between beliefs and actions. Where this becomes problematic, failure is experienced, calling for new treatments of one's identity and for grounding identity in the world. The spiritual–material grounds of one's orientation to the world must be applied to the problem of failure.

APPLYING THE *TOPOS*

I am not suggesting that all rhetoric and god-terms should be analyzed only in light of their spiritual–material themes. The importance of this *topos* lies in the fact that our Western orientation toward the world creates and sustains the dialectical notion of spiritual and material duality. Spiritual–material considerations occur in all institutionalized therapies, religions, *philosophia consolatiae,* cosmology, metaphysics, and even in therapeutic science. Therapeutic rhetoric naturally locates the self in a world of spiritual and material division and merger. Further, since rhetoric is addressed to persons or groups presumed to have their own identities, it seems inconceivable that any such rhetoric could be made that did not regard the incorporeal sense of selfhood or identity. Adherents to particular versions of spiritual–material analysis, such as Christian Scientists, Marxists, evolutionists, business persons, technologists, progressivists, etc., enact formulaic responses to failure as prescribed in their doctrines or beliefs. I was recently told of an incident where a skid-row alcoholic rudely interrupted the sermon at a downtown mission, exclaiming, "This is all really boring!" As the unrepentant sinner was ushered from the room, the astute minister pointed out to his audience: "See, here is proof that the devil is here working among us!" So immersed in his own preaching of spiritual and material division, the minister had no problem transforming this potential failure into evidence for his general thesis about the causes of failure.

We cannot assume, however, that people follow the logic of their chosen spiritual–material presuppositions in consistent ways. Any given person or self-identifying group probably holds spiritual–material interpretations that are prescribed by more than one doctrine. Religious persons can believe in luck, or in fate, and still find their superordinate explanations in religious doctrine. We are all influenced by many interpretations. Further, the pragmatic and situational demands of dealing with failures of various kinds and degrees makes a number of options necessary.

Even though spiritual–material relationships are worked out in grand schemes, everyone must work out ad hoc, situational accounts of life.

Such accounts may be consistent with the general analysis that one embraces, as with the minister I just mentioned, or they may be based upon pragmatic and situational demands that do not conform to one's essential beliefs. There is great room for contradiction when dealing with the contradictions of life, and the many possibilities of the spiritual–material *topos* help people respond to the large variety of contradictory circumstances. When bad things happen to good people, or when there is a tragic accident, we sense contradiction with our belief in the superiority of the spiritual order. At such times we mystify the reasons, taking consolation and finding transcendence in the belief that it is God's will or part of "the plan," or simply could not be helped. The failed fisherman can easily dismiss his earlier boasts and unfortunate results as bad luck, the idea of a spiritual–material interchange quickly consoling him and compensating for his loss without further explanation. In these cases, and in that of the minister, simply evoking the god-terms of a perspective permits apprehension that this is a case of spiritual–material interaction that has meaning in some transcendent sphere; it transforms failure into a kind of success.

There are more difficult cases where coping requires a contradiction between the essential terms of one's view of the world and the actions one must perform. Existential thinkers and dramatists have made their careers by discovering these contradictions and paradoxes. Their analyses commonly show how self–social division is internalized as a problem with self, and is ultimately dealt with in terms of spiritual–material self-division and merger. Such contradictions are often used to debunk the rhetoric of Marxists, who have fought and died for an outcome believed to be inevitable. Contradictions are cited to point up the hypocrisy of religious people who must fight evil for an omnipotent God. Such debunking, however, misses the important, pragmatic fact that people *must* deal rhetorically with the contingencies of experience. Even though a doctrine guarantees inevitable or ultimate success, meaningful life retains the possibility of individual failure. No doctrine applies easily to all cases, else there would be no need for theologians or existentialists. Even for the most doctrinaire persons, failure not only is possible, but their doctrinal systems usually depict it as inevitable and ultimately meaningful. Therefore, even those who adhere to the most sweeping and rigid doctrines need interpretive flexibility and dialectical mobility in order to formulate day-to-day explanations of spiritual–material disorder.

The universal implications and the dialectical nature of spiritual–material formulations allow one to substitute one set of values for another and so transcend the character of experience. Or this character

140

may be transformed by sorting through values and aligning oneself with the greater power. It is often difficult to distinguish transcendence and transformation as functions, since genuine transcendence to another order of value may impart the feeling of transformation of self, and transformation of self may produce the effect of transcending present circumstances.

Because one can always shift the weight given to spirituality and materiality, it is possible that all varieties of material failure can be interpreted as spiritual success, or that all material success can be interpreted as spiritual failing, or even that spiritual success requires material failing. These rhetorical moves are common and reflect the divided self that James analyzed. A person whose self is not divided, who feels personally integrated into social life, is generally able to see spiritual value in material success and material gain in spiritual participation. Failure is then easily compensated and consoled. But one can also *will* a gratifying division of spiritual and material. It is possible for someone pursuing material success to see failure of spiritual goals or values as necessary to material success. Immorality or unethical actions that achieve material goals can be justified in this way. The point is that all experience can potentially be redefined, reinterpreted, and reevaluated, and this allows us to deal differently with different situations, different audiences, and different interpretive contexts—for which spiritualist and materialist alike will at different times have different purposes.

Perhaps the best way to understand why both spiritualist and materialist orientations need active strategies of materialization and spiritualization is to return to the general strategies of consolation and compensation. These, I have said, are the ultimate ends of therapeutic rhetoric. Consolation involves a turning toward the spiritual, or spiritualizing the meaning of a failure in order to find transcendent grounds or a substitute scale of values with which to cope with the failure. Compensation involves a turn toward the material, where a material change or transformation can actualize a balance or erasure of the failure. I have gone to some length to show that in coping with failure, both strategies are necessary and are normally joined. I have shown, too, that an adequate analysis of and response to failure must allow for both strategies. There must be room for transition and movement between the two kinds of relief in order to achieve the ends of therapeutic rhetoric.

Most people are probably neither spiritualists nor materialists in any total fashion. Most people are able to shift values and commitments as cases require. When this is done, spiritual–material alignments are always implicit and often evident. One can find applications of the *topos* in communication and literature treating divorce, home ownership, investment, taxes, death, romance, love, and an infinity of common topics of discourse. On any of these topics one can examine a problem, define it implicitly or explicitly as a conflict between spiritual and material considerations, solve it by counseling alignment with one or the other scale of values, and show how doing so will console and/or compensate either by providing a resolution to the conflict or by discovering a truer interpretation of the problem. Like James, I believe that these functions are of a single genus with diverse options that religions and other spiritual–material doctrines work out on universal scales in treating human failure generally.

Rhetoric dealing with broad social and political problems is also amenable to analysis and treatment in terms of spiritual–material qualities. Whether the problem is the economy, space exploration, medicine, transportation, crime and punishment, law and order, or some other, we assess issues and problems for their degrees of spiritual–material balance. Our effectiveness is often a matter of whether spiritual values are materialized in policy, administration, government, or bureaucracy—all of which are held to be entities that mediate spiritual–material involvements. Spiritual–material themes are often used directly to weigh success and failure, or, as I have said, some summarizing god-term or devil-term may substitute for direct spiritual–material treatment. A policy toward dissidents, for instance, can be spiritually aligned in one fell swoop by designating those dissidents "freedom fighters." This spiritualizes their identities and cause, and it warrants material assistance for a war to actualize spiritual goals we hold in common. One could, however, designate the same dissidents "mercenaries," denying them higher spiritual identity. In this case, one could argue that their materialistic nature warrants withholding ideological and monetary support.

I have tried here to indicate the kinds of uses of spiritual–material themes that can be observed in ordinary dealings with failures and inadequacies. I have also argued that formulations of spiritual–material considerations in doctrines, constitutions, and philosophies both summarize and prescribe kinds of spiritual–material resolutions. Such explicit treatments of spiritual–material problems may, as Emerson and Teilhard illustrated, abstract from experience and common wisdom principles of spiritual–material interaction that can be therapeutically useful in treating individual cases. There are, however, cases where failure is so extreme that serious questions arise about ontological grounds and interpretations. Then spiritual–material relationships may have to be explicitly reexamined and redefined to achieve understanding and treat-

142

ment for failure. This can happen in the thoughts of an individual when one questions one's beliefs and commitments. Or it can happen for an entire nation. Hitler's *Mein Kampf,* Thoreau's *Walden,* or the Declaration of Independence can all be read as reexaminations of the most basic grounds of social existence. We see this kind of discourse in equality movements, religion, therapies for psychic renewal, and treatments of scientific revolution.

Where universal causes and theories are presupposed, yet individuals fail or there is collective suffering, entire belief systems come under scrutiny. Now failures may be redefined as failure of the presuppositions themselves. *Mein Kampf, Walden,* and the Declaration of Independence do just this, as do many other notable treatises. Skinner and Toffler claimed that old principles of spiritual–material ordering must be displaced by new knowledge and new beliefs about the nature of the world. Psychotherapists seek comprehensive reformulations of spiritual–material conceptions as they try to get their clients to transform themselves by seeing themselves and the world differently. Generalization seems possible: When the nature and balance of spiritual–material forces are not contested, one may cope with failure rhetorically by resorting to such commonplace formulations as those expressed in god-terms and devil-terms and in common wisdom. But when basic theories of the spiritual and material forces in the world do not seem to explain failures or allow for their repair, common wisdom and tradition no longer suffice; the rhetoric that copes with failures is then likely to become rhetoric that demands redefinitions of spiritual–material realities and radical revisions of world views, even in coping with small failings. The Boston Massacre involved only a few people, but rhetoric elevated the event to a "massacre" that came to represent the sum total of abuses of the British government. Thus, it came to be written: "When in the Course of human Events, it becomes necessary for one People to dissolve the Political Bands which have connected them with another and to assume among the Powers of the Earth the separate and equal Station to which the Laws of Nature and of Nature's God entitle them. . . ."

The uses of the spiritual–material *topos* in attempts to erase or meliorate human failure differ from those based on self–society and past–future considerations in that drawing upon the spiritual–material *topos* allows one to interpret failings as phenomena occurring within the framework of universal understandings of the world. This allows individuals to interpret their failings as having special significance and to perceive universal solutions for problems. Reformulating one's relationships with spiritual and material forces can make it seem possible to transform oneself, or even the world, through "correctly" aligning belief and action to the redefined realities.

The other *topoi* I have discussed function in coping with failure, but self, society, past, and future can all be spiritualized and materialized. Furthermore, spiritual–material presumptions will always be present when self–society or past–future considerations are employed. Designs of compensation and consolation and goals of transcendence and transformation can be discovered by observing at what points self or society is weighted spiritually or materially, or at what points past or future is depicted as having material or spiritual qualities.

Any comprehensive account of the therapeutic functions of rhetoric must recognize these alternative strategies by which people interpret experience as failure and construct symbolic avenues of repair or resolution. The three pairs of *topoi* I have identified constitute inescapable elements of individual or collective identity. They are the ideational "places" to which we must go to discriminate failure from success and to render disturbing experience intelligible.

However we understand fault and division of self from realities, the grounds for resolving the resulting distress must come through identification of self with universal, orderly, and valued conceptions that allow one to construct a consistent, coherent structure of beliefs, actions, and self-image. We know that people achieve senses of unified selfhood through such identifications, and they do this most often by choosing some self-structure in preference to alternative structures that seem inferior and less satisfying. When our *doings* result in failure, we choose among ways of *being*.

This brings us back to the definitional function of failure with which this book began. The problem of failure is a problem in constructing, reconstructing, and managing identity. Identity can be understood as a rhetorically constructed self-in-relation-to-world. Failure to find such a formulation is failure to identify successfully with one or more elements of *being and doing* in the world. To repair such a problem symbolically is to act rhetorically, and for this we must use ideas and claims that have to do with the *topoi* I have discussed. Therapeutic rhetoric must at some points take into account spiritual and material conceptions that can undergird a stable, consistent, and gratifying sense of selfhood that can be sustained as the experiences of life take their many shapes.

NOTES

1. Eric Hoffer, *The True Believer* (New York: Harper, 1951), 6.

2. William James, *The Varieties of Religious Experience* (New York: Modern Library, 1929), 499.

3. James, 498–99.

4. James, 172.

5. James, 475–6.

6. Mary Baker Eddy, *Science and Health* (Boston: The First Church of Christ, Scientist, 1971), 268–69.

7. James, 163.

8. Karl Marx, *The German Ideology,* in *Karl Marx: Selected Writings,* ed. David McLellan (Oxford: Oxford University Press, 1977), 164.

9. Cynthia E. Russet, *Darwin in America: The Intellectual Response, 1865–1912* (San Francisco: Freeman, 1976), 39.

10. Teilhard de Chardin, *The Divine Milieu* (New York: Harper, 1965), 15.

11. Teilhard, 86.

12. Teilhard, 86.

13. Teilhard, 86–87.

14. Teilhard, 87–88.

15. Teilhard, 88.

16. Ralph Waldo Emerson, "Compensation," *The Collected Works,* ed. Joseph Slater (Cambridge, MA: Belknap Press, 1979), 55.

17. Emerson, 56.

18. Emerson, 76.

19. Emerson, 69.

20. Emerson, 70.

21. Emerson, 72.

22. Plato, *Symposium,* in *The Republic and Other Works,* trans. B. Jowett (Garden City, NY: Doubleday, 1973), 347.

23. Rollo May, "Psychotherapy and the Daimonic," in *Myths, Dreams, and Religion,* ed. Joseph Campbell (New York: Dutton, 1970), 210.

24. Kenneth Burke, *A Grammar of Motives* (Berkeley: University of California, 1969), 108–24; 355–56.

25. Richard Weaver, *The Ethics of Rhetoric* (Chicago: Regnery, 1954), 214.

26. Burke, 105.

27. Weaver, 212–13.

7

A THERAPEUTIC RHETORIC

The chief aim of this book has been to examine failure as a uniquely rhetorical problem. The examination has involved a reconsideration of what failure is and how rhetoric operates when failure is addressed. Several ideas of theoretical and critical importance have emerged, and I shall summarize them here.

RHETORIC AND FAILURE

The central conclusion I advance is that failure and rhetoric are necessarily and fundamentally related. Identification of something as "failure" is itself a rhetorical occurrence. We can fail only in a world where rhetoric operates to assign qualities to the phenomena of life. Still more generally, the objective of making rhetoric is normally to promote some sorts of success and/or to mitigate or forestall some sorts of failure.

It is not remarkable, then, that the recurrence of failure as a rhetorical theme of discourse is striking. In the traditions of Western drama, philosophy, ethics, history, literature, folklore, political and ceremonial speech, and even in science, failure is a central subject of discourse. It is difficult to imagine what literature, broadly conceived, would be like without discussion of failure. Its major forms—the comic, the tragic, and now the tragicomic—represent orientations toward treating the theme of human failure.

Even in their scientific quests, contemporary philosophy and psychology would have little value for us were it not for the possibility of human error and inadequacy. Not even the "hard sciences" are truly independent of the rhetorical theme of failure. Scientific projects and discoveries are formulated and valued because they prevent or redress human mistakes. The possibilities and consequences of failure are typical reasons given for responding to crises, arguing for the significance of research questions and projects, and justifying funding and other support. The social sciences, of course, specially target human failure as their principal domain

147

of interest and inquiry. In all of these circumstances and more, rhetorical tasks must be carried out in defining, analyzing, and evaluating alternative ways of understanding and resolving what are experienced in life as inadequacies.

Typically, past and prospective shortcomings are what generate our interest, so we make and seek discourse that promises to help us, protect us, or otherwise advantage us by offering better ways of being and doing. Said Kenneth Burke, "If [the individual] does not somehow act to tell himself (as his own audience) what the various brands of rhetorician have told him, his persuasion is not complete. Only those voices from without are effective which can speak in the language of a voice within."[1] And what does this "voice within" speak about? About failing and not failing. A person who attends to what is said is always thinking in a frame of reference where personal failures and successes are prominent guides to response. James believed that we could

> take the happiest man, the one most envied by the world, and in nine cases out of ten his inmost consciousness is one of failure. Either his ideals in the line of his achievements are pitched far higher than the achievements themselves, or else he has secret ideals of which the world knows nothing, and in regard to which he inwardly knows himself to be found wanting.[2]

Accordingly, a "voice from without" can best attract interest, involvement, and participation if it speaks in some way about the possibilities of success and failure.

To the great extent that failure is an implicit context for rhetorical exchange, failure becomes the rationale for a vast amount of discourse. Speakers and writers incorporate their audiences' concerns for failure into the symbolism, organization, and dramatic appeal of their works. The critical examinations I have offered in this book illustrate that the very least we can say about themes associated with failure is that they are particularly useful and are universally available means of rhetorically aligning speaker and audience and of motivating consensus as to the meaning, importance, and appropriate responses to any given situation or subject matter.

Failure as a rationale for communication operates in at least the following three ways: (1) Failure is an interpretive way of creating contingency. Matters to be given rhetorical treatment must first be perceived as contingent or subject to change. The prologues of doctrines, the arguments of philosophies, the approaches of leaders, the tricks of spellbinders, the suspense of drama, the plots of narratives, and the enticements of religions and therapies all function to define matters as contingent and to introduce new treatment of those matters. Where we have failed, we will quickly agree that matters are indeed uncertain and potentially threatening. Explicit interpretations of, and implicit address to, perceived or experienced failure thus create a context in which beliefs and actions can be repaired. (2) Identification of failure is a means of persuasion. Individuals attend to what they hear and read because they seek assistance in dealing with contingencies. A possibility of failure invites rhetorical responses; receptivity to persuasion can be created by invoking or creating perceptions and experiences of failure. The pragmatics of these operations have been the subject matter of this book. (3) Creating and resolving perceptions or experiences of failure is thus a form of discourse. Failure must be implicitly or explicitly addressed and in some fashion resolved. Certain rhetorical moves thereby become necessary, not just optional. This, as it were, institutionalizes a form of discourse: a structure that defines failure, locates causes of and responsibilities attending a failure, and remedies that failure by offering new knowledge or beliefs about, attitudes toward, or actions responsive to the failings.

I have noted the frequent occurrence of this form of expression in the basic lore of public address, in the central tropisms of political speech, in the symbols and patterns of narratives in literature and myth, in the doctrines and sermonizings of religions, in theories of interpersonal influence, in scientific cosmology, in social reform, in the psychological theories and therapeutic practices that abound in the many media. In these and other settings, rhetoric very often creates perceptions of failure in order that ideas or matters be attended to, be internalized, and be acted upon by an audience.

I have termed this rhetorical pattern *therapeutic* because in both content and form it functions to treat inadequacies. I have not undertaken to demonstrate exactly how pervasive and significant therapeutic rhetoric is, but I have illustrated the fact that using discourse as curative is a traditional usage in rhetoric and poetics.

Success vs. failure also provides the occasion for criticism. Estimating degrees of success or failure is the warrant for, and provides the rationale for, critical ventures. I have illustrated how failure is codified and operationalized in many critical and scholarly approaches to human events. There is a preoccupation with individual and social failure in critical approaches and their methods. The same can be said for theories about human affairs generally. Theories must account for the data of experience, and what warrants such accounting and what explains such data are very often freighted with concerns for human failure. This I have demonstrated in straightforwardly therapeutic theories, where we should expect such to be the case. I suggest that this is also more true than is commonly recognized in the great breadth of theoretical thought about human concerns.

In sum, it seems impossible to imagine any evaluative thinking or discoursing that is without themes that raise to consciousness concepts of failure and their interpretive significance. Even where discourse seeks to eliminate evaluative considerations, we may always point out that failure is part of the context for interpretations by which individuals and audiences make discourse meaningful for themselves. Any humanly relevant statement about or interpretation of experience can establish or imply grounds for success and failure. What it means to succeed and fail must be understood if we are to discuss *being* intelligibly. In chapter 6 I pointed out that wherever a world view or ontology informs rhetoric, that ontology will provide the grounds for discriminating success from failure. A significant function of rhetoric is to explicate, construct, and apply the meanings and relevances of those dialectical terms. In asking "What is best?" rhetoric answers with criteria for success and failure. This is one reason that it is impossible to construct completely value-free statements about the nature of the human world. Humans cannot speak or listen in a world where there is no concern for failure.

The very existence of rhetoric in the world is a recognition that imperfection can and does exist. In chapter 1 I noted Henry W. Johnstone, Jr.'s remark that "in a society of perfect men, rhetoric would not be needed."[3] I. A. Richards defined the study of rhetoric as "study of misunderstanding and its remedies."[4] Aristotle was more positive when he concluded that rhetoric deals with the contingent, those things which "come the way of all men." That failure figures into his view of contingency is expressed most clearly in his treatment of catharsis through drama. Kenneth Burke wryly observed that the symbol-using animal is "rotten with perfection," meaning that a major function of symbolic activity is performed by perfecting and idealizing what is less than ideal in life, creating universal grounds for the experience and enactment of failure.[5] In sum, rhetoric exists as a response to our perception of flaws. Ricoeur believed that failure is a "rift" in human identity—Johnstone believes that rhetoric is the "wedge" that brings contradictions and the self to consciousness. Rhetoric is the human instrument by which we recognize that failure is possible and at the same time empower ourselves to deal with failure, i.e., to succeed.

150

It does not follow that coping with failure is the only function of rhetoric. I hope to have shown that this function is a more important and prominent function than most people have realized. There are, however, other functions of great importance. Aristotle pointed out that rhetoric serves as an instrument by which humans can weigh the relative expediency of future courses of action. Perelman offered the thesis that epideictic rhetoric is the means by which we preserve and transmit tradition and values. Francis Bacon believed that rhetoric "illustrates" tradition. I hoped to have shown that failure can and often does figure in the themes and forms of rhetoric that accomplish these important functions.

In focusing on the therapeutic functions and form of rhetoric, I have illustrated the broad point that all rhetoric is a means of doing something, and if we ask ourselves what is being done and how, we shall broaden and deepen our conceptions of rhetorical methods. I have asked what rhetoric does therapeutically, how it does so, and what conditions make this function possible. I think it is significant that in its therapeutic functions rhetoric offers compensation and consolation, provides symbolic ways of transforming and transcending self and world, and structures and repairs perceptions and experiences of problems or errors. While I have claimed a certain kind of universality for these functions, I do not claim that these functions in any way exhaust the subject of rhetoric or the general approach I have taken.

A THERAPEUTIC THEORY

The idea that rhetoric has therapeutic benefits is not new. Indeed, the idea is as old as rhetorical study itself. While not a new conception, the idea of a therapeutic rhetoric has much to recommend it in the modern age. The growth of philosophies of self, of psychologism in general, the focus on identity and support in recent social movements, and the therapeutic movement proper all demonstrate that therapeutics are a common form of rhetorical activity in the modern world.

Thinkers have suggested in various ways that ours is a therapeutic age.[6] There is an at least implicit therapeutic focus in much of contemporary scholarship, in paradigms, institutional practices, and individual sense-making of the world. Contemporary philosophy, psychology, sociology, theology, and literary study do seem concerned with finding ways to give us coping knowledge and coping techniques. Business practices, government rhetoric, media drama, therapy literature, therapy cults, support groups, consumerism, and the ethics of success all seem to offer themselves as legitimate ways of forming and transforming self. The individual in possession of and responsible for an identity is the unmistakable target for these rhetorics. I have tried to show that whether new knowledge or new ways of action are sought, these rhetorics are related in that they all operate through treatment of failure. I have proposed that the meaning of this fact can best be gleaned by examining the logical, ontological, strategic, and formulary roles of failure in rhetorical discourse. These roles inform vast amounts of rhetoric, guiding rhetorical content and rhetorical forms. In the Western world this has always been so, but in our therapeutic age the symbolic actions and processes having to do with identity are especially prominent.

I have proposed that there are two fundamental characteristics of our responses to a sense of failure. They are *compensation* and *consolation*. Therapeutic rhetoric undertakes to accomplish remedy through one avenue or the other, and very often offers both in order to provide a complete framework for dealing with failure. Compensation and consolation are rhetorical options. Compensation involves defining failure in such a way that it can be repaired or erased. Consolation entails preparing a respondent to accept a failure that cannot be repaired or completely undone. Loss and the fact of the failure are consolingly interpreted in ways that make the consequences less painful, easier to accommodate, or even valuable according to some alternate set of priorities.

As ways of responding rhetorically to failure, compensation and consolation can be viewed as either ends or means of therapy. They are ends insofar as a particular failure can be successfully compensated or consoled by an appropriate response. Often, however, episodes of failure and their management are not successfully resolved in any complete sense. In politics, interpersonal relations, spiritual life, in one's career, in one's knowledge of self, failures recur. Individual failures must be coped with within a history of failures and despite prospects that further failures will certainly occur. In these circumstances, compensation and consolation become means of coping. A compensatory response may make consolation feasible, or a consolatory response may sufficiently minimize a failure to make compensation easily possible. As I have suggested, religions, world views, and basic orientations toward dealing with life provide sweepingly inclusive frameworks within which compensation and consolation become possible therapeutic applications of knowledge or beliefs.

Achieving compensation or consolation entails interpretive judgment about what failure is being dealt with and how it is to be understood.

This judgment constitutes the rhetorical exigence for therapeutic rhetoric. The judgment stipulates the problem that motivates rhetorical response. But the rhetoric by which we evolve compensation and/or consolation must be created. Its function is to manage failure by repairing failure's causes and consequences or by reinterpreting failure as nonfailure. The self or other that such rhetoric addresses must be persuaded that the reconstructed view of events and prospects can yield greater comfort than could be achieved within the framework of perceptions that existed prior to the rhetorical response.

Certain features are prominent in the uses of compensation and consolation. These schemes are dialectical. They are alternative and distinctive modes of managing failure with discourse, yet they interact in practice. They may be viewed as opposed rhetorical choices, or as potentially conjoined. As options for dealing with failure, compensation and consolation force choices about how a failure is to be defined, interpreted, and subsequently talked or thought about. Yet they also offer rhetorical alternatives for transformation and transcendence through the interpretations they create.

These rhetorical possibilities can be seen in a second feature of compensation and consolation. The dialectical choice between a posture of compensation or of consolation dictates distinctive logical and strategic moves in analysis and action. In consoling, one cannot deny the failure and its significance. One can, however, so exaggerate the failure that it is ultimately a product of such great forces that it can be consoled or compensated on another plane altogether. Likewise, when compensating for a failure one does not have the option of seeing failure as inevitable. Yet one can see the failing as so great that extreme compensations are justified and minor setback are easily consoled.

I have analyzed three pairs of concepts that represent overarching *topoi* used in therapeutic rhetoric. These *topoi* identify the character and meaning of failures—at least in modern Anglo-American culture. The three pairs are *self–society, past–future,* and *spiritual–material*. These pairs identify standard ways of interpreting existential conditions and focusing on significant dimensions. Each topical pair suggests a set of strategic responses to a perceived failure. For example, a failure located as involving conflict between self and society invokes strategies and considerations that are appropriate to self–social management. As *topoi* or ideational "places" where therapeutic themes are found, these headings are potentially tautological. As rhetoric offering compensation and/or consolation is evolved, any line of analysis that uses one pair of these *topoi* can lead to considerations indexed by the other pairs.

The configurations of arguments that are implied by each topical pair constitute logical and symbolic ways of establishing rationales for compensation and/or consolation. Each pair identifies a way of looking at human action and suggests a broad avenue of understanding and response. The three varieties of thematic treatments identified by these pairs appear to encompass the commonplaces of therapeutic rhetoric. They identify the available knowledge or lore about failure; they provide analytic arguments and interpretations.

Considerations of identity are especially prominent in therapeutic rhetoric. These considerations have been dealt with historically as character or personality. "Identity" is a construct we evolve from considering the kinds of relationships and involvements we seem to have with the world. Identity arises from the kinds of successes and failures a person or a group has in the world, and it expresses the knowledge and habits acquired through experience. The *topoi* of therapeutic rhetoric index the ideas, the cultural and strategic resources, that are readily used in generating and maintaining identity in the face of ever-present prospect of success and failure.

Contemporary psychosocial conceptions of identity strongly support the view that identity is rhetorically constructed. Identity is conceived of as a formulated response to basic uncertainties, dissonances, and desires. As I noted earlier, contemporary psychosocial theories of identity are consistent with the rhetorical analysis of coping with failure that I have offered. How self must deal with society, how individual and collective pasts and futures must be made consistent and changed, and how spiritual and ideological life is to be reconciled with mundane existence are the issues that contemporary psychosocial theory addresses therapeutically. Rhetorically considered, these are, of course, the *topoi* I have found in my survey of therapeutic discourse.

We can conclude, then, that developing a case for compensation or consolation serves to rehabilitate a person or group's sense of identity and personal integration. Conceptions of self-worth and social acceptance are repaired by successful response to failure. Discourse offers ways of seeing, knowing, being, and acting that transform self while transcending failure. Very often therapeutic rhetoric conceives that failures are opportunities for self-growth and change, or stimuli for seeing and identifying with higher wisdom or power. Techniques that manage self-social tensions, integrate or explain past–future discrepancies, or reconcile spiritual–material trade-offs and double-binds, construct identities. Guides to identity construction are offered in popular therapies today that urge a new or transformed self. I have tried to point out, further,

154

that these operations of constructing identity are also offered in much political rhetoric, reformist rhetoric, ecological rhetoric, media drama, and popular philosophies.

Modern psychosocial conceptions of identity make clear that identity is an interactive and communicative phenomenon. Criteria such as "effectiveness," "assertiveness," "self-actualization," "success," and "integration" emerge as criteria of self-worth. They imply ethical and rhetorical criteria. Flaws in identity are very often rhetorical flaws that can be solved by a new rhetoric of self. Therapy today offers world views wherein the self allegedly can become indivisible and can reconcile self–social, past–future, and spiritual–material tensions through rhetorical action.

My thesis is that a vast amount of rhetoric is therapeutic in function and design, even where it is not consciously or intentionally so. I believe I have isolated distinctive ideational and formal characteristics of this kind of rhetoric. Arguments and illustrations I have offered and contemporary psychosocial literature support the view that therapeutic rhetoric comes into existence because failure, the sense of having failed, and the expectation that we and others will fail are pervasively with us. The ultimate end of such rhetoric is to persuade those who sense failure that it is possible to reconstruct identity in ways that make failure tolerable; failure can be consoled and compensated. The methods of such persuasion are finite and systematic, not infinitely various nor idiosyncratic. I have sought to identify and elucidate what those methods are and to provoke greater discussion why they are.

NOTES

1. Kenneth Burke, *A Rhetoric of Motives* (Berkeley: University of California Press, 1969), 39.

2. William James, *The Varieties of Religious Experience* (New York: Modern Library, 1929), 134.

3. Henry W. Johnstone, Jr., in *The Prospect of Rhetoric,* ed. Lloyd Bitzer and Edwin Black (Englewood Cliffs, NJ: Prentice-Hall, 1971), 83.

4. I. A. Richards, *The Philosophy of Rhetoric* (New York: Oxford University Press, 1965), 3.

5. Kenneth Burke, *Language as Symbolic Action* (Berkeley: University of California Press, 1967), 3.

6. See, e.g.; Philip Rieff, *The Triumph of the Therapeutic: The Uses of Faith after Freud* (New York: Harper, 1966): Christopher Lasch, *The Culture of Narcissism* (New York: Norton, 1979), esp. p. 33; and Robert M. Bellah, et al., *Habits of the Heart: Individualism and Commitment in American Life* (Berkeley: University of California Press, 1985).

NAME INDEX

157

Name Index

SUBJECT INDEX

160